"*Womb Wisdom* is a book that can reactivate the deep, inherent, often forgotten feminine power within us. Taking Tantra to the next level of unconditional love, appreciation, gratitude, and compassion for all beings, *Womb Wisdom* reveals the union of male and female through the greatest secret that women have: the womb. Woven within the pages is the intimate true-life account of how Anaiya opened the seven gates and five spirals that eventually led to the full opening of her womb. This book is a hands-on practical approach, packed with tools and ways to integrate this wisdom into your everyday lives. *Womb Wisdom* is a vital key to dissolving the problems in modern-day relationships and to entering the mystical chamber of the heart in union with the womb, in relationship. Women and men together as one!"

MARGOT ANAND, AUTHOR OF
THE ART OF SEXUAL ECSTASY

"Padma and Anaiya Aon Prakasha have written a beautiful book that teaches us how to listen to the ancient, creative messages hidden deep within the cyclical powers of the feminine soul. *Womb Wisdom* is a gift of reawakening at this crucial time of great shift upon our planet."

LINDA STAR WOLF, AUTHOR OF *SHAMANIC BREATHWORK: JOURNEYING BEYOND THE LIMITS OF THE SELF*

"*Womb Wisdom* speaks to the soul of all women, revealing ancient teachings that every girl should receive prior to her emergence into womanhood. Through beautiful poetic writing, the authors describe how the womb not only births children but also a woman's spiritual potential, personal healing, and the ability to relate at the deepest level of intimacy. Offering powerful healing meditations, this is an essential read."

CHRISTINE PAGE, M.D., INTERNATIONAL SPEAKER AND AUTHOR OF *2012 AND THE GALACTIC CENTER: RETURN OF THE GREAT MOTHER*

"*Womb Wisdom* activates the spiritual knowledge of the sacred union of the Divine Feminine and Masculine within, catalyzing the birth of a harmonious and evolved consciousness. Through the body-based portal of the womb the reader is provided an invaluable opportunity to integrate shadow and light, access the voice of inner guidance, and emerge anew into divine wholeness."

DANIELLE RAMA HOFFMAN, AUTHOR OF *THE TEMPLES OF LIGHT*

"*Womb Wisdom* brings to the reader and world the hidden (but not secret) power of women, and in particular the womb. Not only is it a profoundly healing read, but it is a delightful read. The authors point to how we "hold the power to weave ourselves into the web of life" and give us the means to do so. This book offers ancient ways to heal the places within and without where we feel separate and divided. The womb, this book shows, holds wisdom for us all."

JULIE TALLARD JOHNSON, AUTHOR OF *WHEEL OF INITIATION*

WOMB WISDOM

Awakening the Creative and Forgotten Powers of the Feminine

PADMA AND ANAIYA AON PRAKASHA

Destiny Books
Rochester, Vermont • Toronto, Canada

Destiny Books
One Park Street
Rochester, Vermont 05767
www.DestinyBooks.com

Text stock is SFI certified

Destiny Books is a division of Inner Traditions International

Library of Congress Cataloging-in-Publication Data

Prakasha, Padma Aon.
Womb wisdom : awakening the creative and forgotten powers of the feminine / Padma and Anaiya Aon Prakasha.
p. cm.
Includes bibliographical references and index.
Summary: "Tools to awaken the creative powers of the womb"—Provided by publisher.
ISBN 978-1-59477-378-5
1. Creative ability. 2. Women—Psychology. 3. Uterus—Psychological aspects. I. Prakasha, Anaiya Aon. II. Title.
BF411.P73 2011
299'.93—dc22

2010038777

Printed and bound in the United States by Lake Book Manufacturing
The text paper is SFI certified. The Sustainable Forestry Initiative® program promotes sustainable forest management.

10 9 8 7 6 5 4 3 2

Text design and layout by Virginia Scott Bowman
This book was typeset in Garamond Premier Pro with Gill Sans and Aries as display typefaces

To send correspondence to the authors of this book, mail a first-class letter to the authors c/o Inner Traditions • Bear & Company, One Park Street, Rochester, VT 05767, and we will forward the communication, or contact the authors at **www.padmaaon.com** or **www.christblueprint.com**.

Contents

PART TWO
The Second Spiral

PART THREE
The Third Spiral

PART FOUR
The Womb of Gaia and Its Guardians

Preface

Padma Aon Prakasha

Womb Wisdom: Awakening the Creative and Forgotten Powers of the Feminine presents information that is not new; rather, it represents a resurfacing of wisdom about the hidden power of women that has been lost and forgotten. This book is written from my experience of initiation into many different sacred traditions and lineage teachings about the womb found in the Indian, Tibetan, Gnostic Christian, Egyptian, and Hebrew sacred traditions. This wisdom was originally part of One Teaching practiced thousands of years ago, before its elements were separated piece by piece into different traditions to preserve their sanctity and the transformative power that they hold. These lineage teachings gave rise to direct experience of the womb and were validated in experiential teachings, healings, and openings of the womb shared in retreats and workshops for thousands of women.

In India, this journey is taken through *smriti* and *sruti,* learning through traditional initiation and wisdom, and then by receiving experiential wisdom through direct revelation once one has mastered a certain aspect of the tradition. This becomes the mainstay of any sacred tradition, for as the teacher begins to teach, more is given to the teacher by the lineage to share.

I have been initiated over the past thirteen years to bring all these pieces of Womb Wisdom back together again. My journey has taken me to more than sixty countries, to hundreds of sacred sites known and unknown, and to many teachers, most of whom are not known, some of whom even have no names, and all of whom have no wish to be known in the world at large.

These journeys involved the deepest forms of sitting meditation and shamanic ritual in sacred sites, from the heart of the Aboriginal deserts of Australia to the fertile druidic lands of Ireland and from within the stone circles of England. From delving deep into the light and shadow of tantric relationships, to exploring the depths of the body and the power of the life force and light force in Egypt, or becoming aligned to the healing of the heart and soul in the south of France, it has been my role to be initiated into these lineages, to meditate to receive the wisdom of the lineage, so that I might share it in a form accessible and understandable for you today.

Lineage transmissions are not linear. Once one is authentically initiated, one's life changes drastically, and one can receive all the accumulated wisdom of the lineage from thousands of years. This is authorized by the elders of that tradition, many of whom have passed on from their bodies into the spirit world.

Before I could teach others, I had to fully experience. My experiences in the mystic arts began with my initiation at age two into the Brahmin lineage, then beginning to read the Bhagavad Gita at age four, followed by the Koran, the Bible, and the European philosophers by age seven. At age twenty-one, an experience of God Consciousness changed my life forever.

Shortly after this, I was initiated by the Divine Mother in India. In this initiation, I was led to an ancient temple high up in the Himalayas. As I entered the sanctum of the temple and went up to the altar, hundreds of people swarmed around me, chanting *"Jai Ma, Jai Ma!"* ("Praise be to the Mother, Praise be to the Mother!") in a raucous yet joyful celebration and plea. As I stood before an ancient yet simple carved effigy of the Mother, gazing innocently at Her face, everything stopped around me. All sound, all other people vanished from sight, as I was granted an audience with Her.

I stopped in this silence. All I heard was, "What do you wish for?" This was repeated three times, and I understood that I could ask for anything at this moment: anything I desired, any boon, would be granted if I but asked for it. All that came to my heart, all I could say, was, "I wish to serve you, Mother." As soon as I said this, a priest came up to me, placed a garland of flowers around my neck, and gave me some *prasad* (an edible offering), sweetmeats, to consecrate the offering I had given of myself.

This then opened the doorways to my becoming initiated into Saivite Tantra and its knowledge of the womb and Shakti, the feminine life force, through the head priests of Kedarnath, Badrinath, and Pashupatinath, and into the Sama Veda through the Arunachala sampradaya, among others. Perhaps the most powerful initiations came through Sri Om, an awakened teacher in the lineage of the Buddhist Master Tsongkhapa and Buddha Maitreya, after which I sat in *samadhi,* the highest form of meditation, and the goal of meditation, for two months.

Shortly after this, I was led to Hawaii in 1997. I was doing yoga at a yoga studio when I was asked to give an offering of some teachings to some women. I responded that I would, expecting a handful of women to turn up. Twenty women showed up, and in a whirlwind of three hours they cried, released, and opened their wombs to such effect that I realized there was something important happening here that was very precious, and much needed.

My main initiations into Tibetan Tantra with two female teachers, and their wisdom and experiential practices regarding the womb, helped to show me the Pulse of Life held within all women, the heartbeat of birth. This was then added to by my initiations into the Order of Melchizedek and the Gnostic Christian Lineage of Magdalene, as I related in my book *The Christ Blueprint* (NAB 2010). This lineage shared much with me about how the womb holds love in its depths and how important it is to reeducate men and women on the importance of it. These practices now are being used by thousands of women and men to great effect in Shakti Circuit retreats and workshops the world over.

Writing this book required me to spend years immersing myself in the womb and experiencing its depths, particularly with my beloved Anaiya, whose womb opened and shared with me the depths of love. The very ability to create this book arose from male and female union, which is part of the goal of Womb Wisdom, and it is through our union that this book, many years in the making, could finally come out in a contemporary way for you today.

The importance of this information being revealed to humanity at this time cannot be more urgently stressed, for as we race headlong into 2012 and beyond, more and more of us are experiencing strange ascension symptoms, or evolutionary changes in our biology and consciousness as we change rapidly, and as the earth, too, changes rapidly.

The ways to birth ourselves and the earth through these strange and new phenomena are found in the womb and ways of being that are gradually being reintroduced again to us all. Humanity is maturing, and as enough people reach the emotional and spiritual status of adults rather than teenagers, more of this timeless wisdom can emerge.

Today, all the mystical traditions are opening the doors to their secrets in order to accelerate the transformation in those who genuinely desire it and are committed to doing the deep inner work required to accomplish this noble goal.

Womb Wisdom contains some wisdom known already in the world, and some not already known. In reading this book, you are invited to explore the missing pieces found through the direct and experiential connection with the womb. This book is experiential: it is based on real transformative experiences that people have. What is needed now is the return of the power of Woman, as simple as it is profound, and this is the reason this book and these teachings are being shared, taught, and released again on Earth.

Womb Wisdom is ancient yet timeless, as it applies to all human beings, regardless of caste, color, race, or religion. Its truths have been practiced before and are held in many lineages, having support from them in their resurfacing again in the world. Yet they are universal in nature, as they go to the core of creation and the human experience, touching on birth and death through the feminine flow of the life force, free and loving, without boundary, concept, and ideas. Some parts of *Womb Wisdom* overlap with a previous book of mine, *The Power of Shakti,* but I felt it was important that parts of *The Power of Shakti* were included here in order to provide a more complete womb library and reference.

Simple and unique to each person, *Womb Wisdom* can free you of need and bring you into unconditioned love by allowing you to give. This is perhaps the greatest gift of all.

Preface

Anaiya Aon Prakasha

My journey began when I was twelve years old. I was walking out of Sacré Coeur Cathedral in Paris when I saw a "beggar" sitting on the steps, head down with his hands out, as if asking for something. I was holding my father's hand, and yet my head kept turning back toward this man, until finally my fire arose, as I wriggled myself free, because I simply had to run to him.

I placed my hands over his as he raised his head slowly to gaze into my eyes. As our eyes met, I knew I was looking into the deepest expression of love on the planet. What was this? I was suspended, I was taken, and life, as we say, was never ever the same again. I had seen the face of God, the heart of Christ.

This experience stayed with me for the rest of my life as a beacon, a candle of light flickering in my darkest moments. From that moment on, I was walking the Path of the Beloved, and every ounce of my incarnation was given as an expression of love. As I matured, waves of *bhakti* (devotion) raged through my body, and I had no clue what I was supposed to be doing with all this energy.

I came across kundalini yoga in 1996 and never looked back. My first class was a powerful recognition and remembrance of both *Shakti* (life force) and *Bhakti* (loving devotion). Through this tradition I was given the knowledge on how to stimulate and balance the internal subtle energies of the body, mind, and soul. I practiced long and hard to strengthen my Shakti and deepen my character in the exterior world. I worked on the glitches within my personality and endeavored to create an established, committed, and powerful woman. I studied the subtle anatomy, the tendencies of mind, and how to develop awareness. I was consumed with passion, aliveness, and inspiration, yet something was missing . . . someone to share that with.

In 2006, I took a Bodhisattva vow in the Tibetan tradition to give my entire life to the service of others, to leave no rock unturned, and by any means necessary to love, serve, and remember. I prayed to meet my beloved in this lifetime. With my passion I knew this was possible. I never ever wished to meet my beloved and simply be with him and live happily ever after. Oh, no, my prayer was to meet him, and together in our union, *share* this great love with everyone. It was about giving everything from that union.

As I began to teach kundalini yoga, there was a frenzy of energy. People swarmed to the classes, I was asked to write a book by the publishing house Harper Collins, I was invited to teach and speak all over the world. I gave my everything to these teachings, and the focus of my work was the freedom to love. Every class ended with love, that freedom, and that invitation to step into the greatness of giving. The classes and retreats were euphoric, waves of ecstasy consumed people, and there were times when I felt a revolution was being born.

Almost every person I taught was female, which is unusual, as kundalini yoga attracts mainly men in the West. My intention was to restore vitality and beauty within women, to strengthen their glandular and nervous systems so that they would have the power to maintain the preservation of life when the going gets tough. I focused on clearing their sexual past and wounds of love, inspiring in them the desire to love at greater depths.

And then . . . along came Padma, and within moments I realized I had left an enormous piece of the puzzle out—the womb, and the shadow. Through his grace I have come to meet, commune with, and embrace both. When writing this book with Padma, I was moving through the process of opening the womb, I developed the first stages of cervical cancer, among a few other health issues within my reproductive system. By the time the book was finished I was completely healed and restored back to full health. I have made sure that this healing process is richly transcribed within these pages to help support others who may have to pass through this gateway. So, from this unified beingness, I bring you my piece of the puzzle as a living example of the womb, and of love.

Introduction

The Creator gathered all of Creation and said,
"I want to hide something from the humans until they are ready for it. It is the realization that they create their own reality."
The eagle said, "Give it to me. I will take it to the moon."
The Creator said, "No. One day they will go there and find it."
The salmon said, "I will bury it on the bottom of the ocean."
The Creator said, "No. They will go there, too."
The buffalo said, "I will bury it on the Great Plains."
The Creator said, "They will cut into the skin of the earth and find it even there."
Grandmother Mole, who lives in the breast of Mother Earth, and who has no physical eyes but sees with spiritual eyes, said,
"Put it inside of them."
And the Creator said, "It is done."

Hopi Creation Story

We come forward now at the brink of a quantum shift, but what is it? What is this evolutionary shift of which we are all on the brink? Could an important part of it be about women regaining their loving power and channeling it into the right places?

Maybe we have just forgotten where to channel it. The deepest, most ancient secrets of life lie within the womb of every woman. The womb is the holiest temple in your body, the most energy-filled place in your body, the place from where your inner voice, deepest guidance and clarity, stillness, creative expression and power arise. It is your primordial voice and connector into the web of life, the web of interdependence that connects all living beings to each other.

We are all birthed from the womb, yet it is one of the least known parts of ourselves. This is not surprising, for it holds the greatest power that a woman possesses: the power to nurture, grow, and create new life. This power of creation is what each woman holds, but usually only exercises in the process of giving physical birth.

The womb is not just a place to give birth to a baby; it is a place and state of being that births *us,* that births new realities, that holds a power for deep transformation for ourselves and for others with whom we come into contact. The womb is a woman's feminine core, the generator of tremendous creative potential, vitality, boundless well-being, sensual power, and manifestation. It not only births children but also the fullness of feminine spiritual potential, personal healing, and the depths of relating for which we all yearn. It births and unifies the divine masculine and feminine, bringing balance and loving power to our deepest relationships. The heart does not do this alone: it does it in alliance with the womb.

Imagine it: there is a place within us that holds the power of life and death, yet we only use it once or twice in our lifetime. The rest of the time it lies neglected, its power hidden, misunderstood, and forgotten about.

Yet this has not always been so. In the past, and in present-day indigenous traditions, women have known the way of the womb, the knowledge, practices, and power of the womb, and how to use it to create and love on a profound level. Some of these great women from both East and West include Mary Magdalene, Mother Mary, the female Buddha Yeshe Tsogyal, the priestesses of Isis, the Daoist and African sisterhoods, and the druid shamanesses of Ireland and England.

As women, we have become so divorced from the womb, our primal center of gravity, joy, creativity, and soul connection, that we have forgotten who we are and how we could be. Instead we try to compete on masculine terms and conditions to get by in the world of today. The flowering of the feminine rose has become dwarfed by the pillar of the masculine, instead of both sitting side by side in harmony and relative equality.

This imbalance is caused by our forgetting about the womb and its true purpose and power. In this forgetting, men too have forgotten how to relate fully to the feminine and how to be truly human, building walls of intellectual justification and anger around the wounds and holes that have been created by this separation. Many religions and ways of behavior have been influenced by this separation, creating a grossly distorted view of spirituality and social behavior that has formed the current infrastructures of society and informs how we are living life today. These structures have been created by a handful of men without women, creating in turn an innately flawed, imbalanced worldview and society.

The effects on human society of this imbalance are many and manifold, impacting every area of human life, from the environment, to nuclear arms, educational and cultural values, spiritual traditions and commandments, the loss of family values, and the failure of many intimate relationships between man and woman. In short, the loss of Womb Wisdom has created a huge imbalance on planet Earth that impacts all of us, creating an unstable foundation for our cultures and our lives that is threatening to topple over at any moment, so lopsided has it become.

The increase of intellectualization allied with a lack of actual womb experience means that women have been finding their center of gravity in their heads, rather than in their wombs and hearts. This arises partly as a reaction to the male-dominated ideas and concepts that form the foundation of most religions and societies today.

A woman's center is in her womb-heart, not her head. She lives on Earth, connected through relationship, not in an abstract concept or code of what life is. As soon as a woman's center of gravity shifts to the womb, she becomes centered, empowered, present, and grounded. When a woman's center is in her head, she suffers badly and becomes more disempowered, trying to compete with men who are mind centered, thereby losing connection with her feminine essence.

Women are sad that they are centered in their heads, as they innately know that it is not true for them. When they start doing womb work, their sadness and rage well up within them as they realize this, and they start to shift their centers of gravity and resonance back to their primal center, the source of their joy and womanhood. This then allows the heart to flower, deeply and organically, flowing in spontaneity, emanating from the web of life, from all that nurtures and supports life.

For thousands of years women have been without a role model, not knowing where to turn, or whom to look to for inspiration and nurturing. Women have not known where to belong, and the changing roles imposed upon them by a reason-driven society have further pushed the essence of the feminine nature into seclusion, creating a pastiche of true femininity. This is easily seen in modern-day consumer society where this pastiche is used to sell products, seduce, and manipulate.

Deep within, you know that you must go beyond cultural and acceptable norms in order to stand in your own authority. Nothing of greatness is achieved without going beyond the norms of the day, in any field of endeavor. Woman becomes able to accomplish her own birthing when she leaves behind her attachment to the collective consciousness, the traditional institutional beliefs of what is considered in the collective to be culturally acceptable womanly roles and virtues.

In this separation, you become able to truly trust yourself and what is uniquely individual to you. This process of transformation depends upon your ability to feel and fully experience essential feminine values birthed from the womb. Merely having knowledge of them or understanding them rationally is not enough. You have to experience the feminine, making it your own, and living fully in this initiation, holding your deep-felt belly wisdom and gut knowing, your gut instincts to preserve and keep life going.

All life benefits when women come to love their bodies and live from their truth. For the womb is the generator and keeper of Life, the source of full feminine expression. The womb and ovaries are the light generators of the feminine, and the creators of joy. When they are cleared, when they are healed of wounds, those many veils of disempowerment, miseducation, and repression, a woman may connect fully with her own feminine core in clarity, joy, and the full, free expression of the life force, the orgasmic energy of bliss.

Activating the womb is a powerful act that heals many deep-seated, age-old wounds in both the female and male consciousness. Healing the womb helps activate and illuminate the collective psyche and also powerfully heals on the personal level. For when the womb is cleared, healed, and restored in connection to the heart, women come into their full power. By doing so, the men too become balanced, whole, and healed, as this feminine fire holds the crucible and container for heart-centered relationships.

By women living from their center of power, joy, and life-nurturing capacities, and men supporting this, both become deeply nourished through this deepening and opening within themselves. When a woman and a man have integrated both their aspects, they can rise above being just one or the other, realizing that male and female are just roles to be played, like putting on a robe to suit different occasions. The fluidity of moving between these polarities is accessed when a woman is totally able to be a woman, and a man a man.

An awakened, socially conscious, and egalitarian society is built on the foundation of the womb that honors life in all its forms as the basis of society, not as an "add on" or a pleasing secondary thought. This divine design is activated and manifested through the organic flowering of the womb and application of its laws and rhythms. This divine design descends soul energy into manifestation; at present, human civilization descends mental energy into manifestation and ascends root chakra or survival/power/sexual issues into manifestation.

With enough open and healed wombs, no war would dare be fought by men who listen to the voice of the womb, to the empowered, life-affirming woman in their life who shares the sustaining, nurturing power of life. Poverty would be wiped out if more female leaders created, shared, and distributed structures for people to become self-empowered and to live in real relating.

The strengths and depths of the womb provide the security and foundation deep within for us to rise up and express ourselves freely through the heart. The head and heart work within grounded foundations sunk deep within the womb. The head by itself cannot come into the heart. The womb is required to bring down the mind into our true center, and then the mind can rise up and express through the heart from solid foundations.

The womb feels autonomous, has a voice of its own, and can respond depending on what is required in each moment. The womb's voice is wise, ancient, powerful, and connected to the primordial. It is sunk deep, whereas the heart gives rise to passion, inspiration, and the giving and expression of love. Womb holds, heart gives. Heart's desire is to unify and bring things together—to end division. The womb holds the space, the container, the crucible for this to happen, for this to birth into manifestation.

Heart manifests womb, and womb holds heart in a secure space, allowing the heart to go deeper into its layers rather than just being on the surface or on a sentimental aspect of the heart. The womb holds the steadiness, the unwavering center and ground of creation, steady, still, reliable—the well of creation. With this foundation, the heart then feels safe and secure, feeling its innate and natural ground to lean, rest, and rely upon, a place to arise from in wisdom and strength, able to see clearly and give accordingly to what is the highest potential in that moment.

One can say that the womb is the bank of the river, and the heart *is* the river. The womb is the container for the alchemy of love to occur and rise into manifestation and being. Mind is the servant of womb-heart, designed to carry out its orders. The heart is incomplete without the maturity of the womb. The womb establishes itself deep within the character, the clarity, the stillness and the inner guidance, the commitment and stamina, housing the ground upon which you may come to take solace and guidance throughout your greatest tests in life.

You have within you this reliable source of stillness. Do you have the heart to discover it? If so, this book will help you.

Inside *Womb Wisdom* you will discover:

- How the mysteries of creation are encoded within each woman's body
- How to become your own guru and guide through the womb
- How the five spirals of the unfolding of the womb form a Cosmic Woman
- How to find your own map to your womb in the Womb Mandala
- Meditations to ignite the Pathways of the Womb
- Information about the seven gates to activate your sacred, sensual self
- The voice of your womb, womb dialogues, and how you can access this voice
- Why men need the womb to step into the Divine Masculine
- The sacred sites of the womb around the world

To facilitate this essential work, this book also contains a CD titled *Life Cycles: The Essence of the Womb*. It provides a rich tapestry of a soundscape full of the beauty, power, and soul of sacred traditions worldwide, allied with psychoacoustic frequencies designed to take you deep into the journey of creation, life, death, and rebirth. This CD will facilitate your process of opening your womb.

Womb Work is designed for you to grow and bloom this holy place within into full manifestation. With the resurrection of the womb comes the resurrection of man. Man will find a new identity that is his timeless, primordial identity, his true identity, when he comes into harmony with the clear and activated womb-heart.

So men . . . stand up and support the women in your life! Do not be scared that you will lose your power, for you will in fact gain the greatest power of all: love born through humility, that which makes a real man, a king and leader to suit your queen and guide. Have faith, and listen to the womb; it will serve you to enter truth, the greatest bliss, the greatest softness, and the deepest power, the wisdom of which will make you a real man.

Women, delve deep into your primal power, beyond the appearances, customs, and religions of this day. Delve into the knowing that you have always had and always will—a knowing that no religion can ever encompass and that no culture can ever define. Delve deep into your belly and the brain that lies there: the primal brain, your original voice, the voice that will never betray you and will always lead you to the truth of love in action, the being of joy, and peace: The Voice of Life itself.

PART ONE

The First Spiral

1
Accessing and Healing Stored Unconscious Emotions

Melting the Masks

Science is now discovering that more neurons fire in our bellies than our actual brains. There are in fact 72,000 nerve endings in our bellies, whereas only 50,000 are found within the brain. In Chinese medicine, the small intestine (part of the womb circuit) is the place that stores the deeper emotional issues from our hearts, and in Tibetan medicine it is the center for affection and bonding.

At this point in the first spiral, one has not mastered emotions in order to see the bigger picture because the emotions stored in the womb have not been contacted or accessed consciously. Womanly discernment, clarity, and intuition are just beginning to develop. One can be swayed and controlled by appearances and by others, as a foundation is not yet formed, and if it is, it is formed upon the basis of the mind.

We start to delve deeper into the wounds on the first spiral of the womb with the onset of a personal crisis. We may feel called deep within us, in an inexplicable and mysterious way, to the womb once we hear about it. We may be searching for answers and trying out all kinds of approaches, none of which get to the core of our felt sense of something missing, with all other approaches not seeming to work to bring us into this deep place we *know* exists within us.

For most women today, a womb is an organ just like the rest of the organs that give life to our bodies and minds. Just as with the heart, liver, gallbladder, kidneys, we all know the womb is there, but do we give any thought to it other than when we think of menstruation or pregnancy? What else is it there for? What if we asked the questions: What else does my womb do other than give birth? What is the wisdom and power within my womb?

Ask yourself this question honestly: Do you find a part of your life to be unfulfilled, lacking in something you cannot quite put your finger on?

The way of the womb is for the woman who wants to be totally empowered as a woman, manifesting her soul mission, and being able to have intimate, fulfilling sacred relationships, actively participating and engaging fully in the spontaneous joy and wave of life. It is for that woman who wishes to fully claim her authentic self as a live and flowing experience, and live her womanhood totally, without reservation or hesitation, without having to compromise. It is for that woman who wishes to have an open, fulfilling sexual life, and who wishes to use this energy to dynamically fuel her evolution, health, and lifestyle.

The womb is an honest mirror of the soul, serving to reflect the truth about the progress that is being made in our growth. It is flowing, cooling, gentle, and mothering like a calm ocean, cooling and balancing pools of excess masculine attitudes and expressions.

WOMB CONNECTION THROUGH THE MOON TIME

The experiences of pregnancy and the menstruation or moon cycle are the first gateways, the first stirrings that are offered to you to tap in to the womb's creative juices and rich depths. The womb is usually forgotten about unless it is carrying a child, and then it is the child that kicks its feet and beats its tiny fists against its walls to remind you that it is there. Once a month is the only time when our hands press against the womb as we cry out in pain, when menstrual cramps call for our attention. I am amazed when I hear women clutch their wombs as they bend forward exclaiming, "Ah, my stomach!"

These cramps are a calling to bring your attention fully into the center of the womb. These pains are an ally, a way back, and into, the wisdom of the womb. The next time you try to numb the pain, think again. Use the physical sensation as a vehicle to draw you in, and deep. I assure you, you will never look back.

In fact, many women try to control or stop the rhythm of their menstrual moon cycle by swallowing pills rather than experience their moon cycle during a holiday or other inconvenient time. This halts your connection to the flow of the cycles of life and death that are expressing themselves through you. The next time you think to take some pills or patches to halt your menstrual cycle, think again. You are denying yourself your femininity for the sake of convenience and buying into modern-day fast-food consumer society. You are becoming more man than woman.

The blood time or moon time is a time to go within, to feel and see the messages and visions that the womb has for you in her attunement to the oceans, the moon itself, and the blood that gives life. When you bleed, your focus shifts, and you become more internal. The reference points you use to guide yourself become more fluid as you enter a different, darker world that is asking for your exploration, asking you to let go of your rational side, your mental stability. Here, you are being asked to not simply observe life but to immerse yourself in its immense power deep within you.

This is the darkness inside, and it is there whether we bleed or not. It is just in the bleeding time that we get a glimpse of this uncontrollable, untamable part of ourselves.

The moon time is a time of retreat, of sanctuary, to rest and immerse within, to find that space within that shelters, and also hides, part of you. This time can bring your relationships closer and bring lovemaking to another level of sanctity and honoring, for to let a man into your blood deeply touches both of you when he is honored as such. Indeed, the tantric Bauls of Bengal have an exquisitely crafted science of the blood cycle, detailing the peaks and troughs of the five days, and the best times to make love, which lie on the fourth day in particular.* For you are more vulnerable, more honest, more open with how you feel beneath the surface, beyond the everyday, for you are closer to the source of your strength, your power, your vulnerability, and your feminine essence.

In the moon time, we become more attuned to nature, to shifts in mood, to sound, to energy movements. More things can irritate us as we try to come to grips with our shadow. We tolerate less and withdraw more, following instincts and desires more keenly. Yet we try to block all this, continuing as normal, putting up a facade, fitting into the everyday, distracting ourselves from the pain and the feelings, staying external, trying to remain useful for what we think is required of us. Nothing is further from the truth. What is needed is for you to follow these urges, to withdraw, to not conform, and to be what you need to be, not what others need you to be.

We have noticed that the worst cases of PMS are in women who feel suppressed, repressed, or have womb woundings. The moon cycle reveals the wounds, the expectations, the things we do not like or want to do but which our minds have been telling us we must do. The womb is the opposite of the mind; she listens not to reason but to feminine truth, and it is up to you to follow this. If you do not express what is hidden behind the pain and the irritation, then it will play out in different ways within you and in your relationships.

---

*A good source for further information on this subject is *The Place of the Hidden Moon* by Edward C. Dimock Jr. (Chicago, Illinois: University of Chicago Press, 1989).

The moon time is a gift to reveal where you are not being true to yourself and where you are investing your energy in the false. The rage, the grief, the fear, the irritation, and the despair is simply blocked energy of the shadow that the blood cycle rises up to reveal, and then it is up to you to explore, express, release, and reveal what has been lurking underneath, waiting for this moment to be seen. And this is the suppressed creativity of the blood cycle unleashed: doing what your womb wants to do.

Embracing Your Shadow in the Moon Time

Once a month you get to see and meet your shadow directly. When journeying through the womb, this monthly encounter will become worth its weight in gold. Your personal shadow—and for some, possibly the whole collective of womankind—can be accessed and moved through. There have been a number of times when I hear myself and others exclaim, "This is so unlike me, totally out of character. I can't understand why I just said/did that." You are right; you can't understand the transformative power of this shadow self that takes hold of you for periods of time.

When the shadow is at the helm, the unconscious woman will not even realize that she is being controlled by her shadow. Yet the great work is to spot instantly the moment you become disturbed and irritated. The shadow awakens. It is time to feel and sense its impression within your body and to inquire what it really wants and needs. The innocence contained within the shadow, at the core of its being, has a healing and empowering message, which it wants to share with you. Its needs are keys into the deeper openings of the shadow and the beginnings of a lasting dialogue and loyal friendship.

The womb begins to open further when you consciously embark on this journey into the feminine self and your own empowerment. This happens when you acknowledge and accept that you are not a victim, and have never been a victim, but a powerful creator of *all* your experiences. It is the first realization that nothing has been done to you. This is a humbling experience.

Self-responsibility and self-empowerment go hand in hand. Once you accept you have created all that has happened to you in order that you might learn and grow, then you can truly unravel and heal both personal and collective wounds. It is here that women tap in to their real feminine strength and access the will to feel what was previously rejected within. Through willingness and courage to face directly what is/was unpleasant or painful, through this embrace, the dormant womb can begin to emerge and flower.

Anything unfelt, ignored, denied, or avoided has to arise so you can access your true self.

There are a multitude of strategies that we have acquired to protect ourselves. To avoid unpleasant or overwhelming feelings we create ways in which to block them out and get by. It actually takes more energy and effort to keep the lid on this hurt and pain than it does to take the lid off and be free.

We do this first by contracting our bodies, holding our breath and bellies in tightly, constricting and holding this posture of protection to disguise and avoid feeling. These unpleasant or uncomfortable feelings remain stuck in our wombs and can often keep us bound our whole lives, as we avoid and resist the very emotions that can liberate us.

When these are fully felt and traveled through, a sense of empowerment, sustained energy, and a feeling of wholeness, of integrity, can arise. The feeling of something missing or a sense of something lacking or being deficient can also disappear.

Not embracing emotions leads to fear, turmoil, and unrest. This emotional stress is held in the womb and in the digestive and anal pathways. By an embrace of emotions, and the often difficult path they create, joy, beauty, and peace are found. Soothed, healed emotions allow us to live life in surrender and to be happy without attachment. If you find it hard to surrender, and find it hard to be happy without attachment to a person, situation, place, or thing, then there are blocks in the womb, for opening to the joy of soulful emotion is the language of the feminine spirit.

 Basic Womb Connection

Touching and massaging the womb helps you to focus on it by placing your hands over her and breathing into her. Try this now.

1. Sit comfortably on the floor with the soles of your feet together and your knees spread. This is an important posture that enables you to sit on your throne, centered in your power.
2. Close your eyes, hold your hands over the womb in an inverted triangle, and breathe down into her. Focus and meditate. You may choose to allow sounds from the womb to arise and spontaneously express themselves. Just let go into it. You will be surprised at what she needs to share and say.

When you start to open the first spiral of the womb, physical and emotional purification happens. Physical discharges and deep emotional release cleanse the womb on a cellular level as it starts to bloom and flower.

WOMB CONNECTION THROUGH TRUE SEXUAL EXPRESSION

The womb's wounds are comprised of the memories and emotions that create our mistrust of life and others and that impair a woman's level of creativity, inspiration, stability, success in loving relationships, and fertility. Allowing the deep wellsprings of grief, pain, the masks of hardness, indifference, and the veneers of cynicism and fragility to melt is the first step in healing the womb.

This initial thawing affects every aspect of life, but in particular we can notice it through our lovemaking and sexual expression. In the first spiral of the womb, you may find it difficult to experience full orgasm. You may feel a sense of holding back, of pain or sadness arising, of frustration, of superficial pleasure, of not being totally present, of feeling unfulfilled but not speaking up. You may even enjoy the act of making love but feel that it has reached its apex and that the experience always tends to feel the same. Something else is beckoning to you, an ancient memory deep within your core, a whisper of something beyond your experience, but something you know intimately.

When the womb is clear and free from restrictions, a new discovery of orgasm can be allowed, experienced as a natural release of free expression. These could be orgasms of vaginal release, or full-body orgasms that are felt as rushes of bliss coursing throughout the whole being, or orgasms felt in the womb, heart, and subtle bodies. There are as many different types of orgasms as there are stars in the sky. They cannot be limited by definition or comparison to other women.

The immune system relies on being supported and fed by your sexual energy, 90 percent of which feeds directly into our immunity. So in essence, without a thriving and vital flow of sexual energy, your defense system will be undernourished, leaving you prone to sickness, weakness, and depression. An orgasm, when flushed throughout the entire bodymind, has the sustenance to bring in a complete healing state. Try this next time you are ill and see what happens.

When you live in this stream, you live according to your heart's desires, your innermost urging and true calling, following your inner voice and listening to your natural rhythms as they harmonize with the earth, your loved ones, the cycles of time and rhythm, and life itself. The life spark within all of us, birthed from the womb, pushes toward this movement, the very movement of creativity, joy, and free sexual energy. These movements constantly go through you and the earth and are made conscious when your emotional state is agile and you can easily emote, for emotion equals energy in motion.

To align to the movements of the womb requires that you become fluid. When you are fully fluid, you can experience any feeling whatsoever at any time, at will. Thus if you can, at will, feel delight, love, anger, or tears without attachment to them, then you can be moved by Spirit, which is always fluid and open. However, the less you can summon feelings, the more you are frightened of them, the more you are at their mercy. Conversely, the more you allow yourself to experience feelings, the less you can be enslaved by them. If you allow them to pass through you, you become transparent, without holding on to anything or anybody.

Thus you learn to move the body, feelings, and mind, so that spirit can move you. In this flow, you feel you are in sync with everything within and around you. The world and your relation to it seems different . . . it is as if you are involved with the process of creation, instant by instant. You are creating it as it is creating you; for it is always there, you just are too busy to notice it.

Have you ever noticed when you ask for something and it magically appears within a day or an hour? This is living in the flow, for it is already happening; it is manifesting through you.

HEALING THE BROKEN CONNECTIONS

Delving bravely into the broken connections found in the first spiral and loving the hell out of them creates a sense of confidence in your ability to heal yourself and live the truth of who you are. The healing does not end in this spiral but begins the journey of the womb, an ever-deepening journey into the mystery and awe of the vessel of life, a place for growth, transformation, generation, creativity, and of birth to our own self, to our own fulfillment, to our own wholeness.

Embarking on this journey, you can start to rediscover your own latent gifts and gain a deeper sensitivity, a deeper knowing of what you are here for. These gifts may not, however, be tempered by maturity; one could say that you are like a teenager starting to access the delights and pitfalls of entering into the fertile power where you create according to your heart-womb's desires. The following is an exercise to help you get in touch with your own true self.

The Womb Dialogue Practice

In the first spiral of the womb, you may discover many things about yourself. To help you discover what is happening, take a deep breath down into your womb, your own sacred cave. Place your hands there and ask these questions:

- Are you disease-free in your belly, womb, and sexual organs?
- Have you had any major surgery that involves your belly and womb?
- What is your mother's story with her body and sexuality?
- Do you suffer from PMS or hormonal imbalances?
- Do you feel emotionally clear about your birth story? That is to say, were you born through a cesarean section, through the force of forceps, were you induced or premature, was the umbilical cord tied around your neck, was the birth traumatic, what drugs were used, was your mother in danger, were you adopted?
- Do you feel any impact now from your birth story?
- Did you ever have an opportunity to grieve an abortion, a miscarriage, or a stillbirth?
- Have you suffered sexual, emotional, or physical abuse in your life?
- Are you able to recognize how you may abuse or punish yourself by your internal dialogue or your actions?
- Do you enjoy making love?
- Are you completely open and receptive to being penetrated by a lover?
- Do you hold back pleasure or sound when making love?
- Are you able to love your body, your womanhood, in total acceptance?
- Do you have orgasms? Are your orgasms full-bodied?
- Do you trust the masculine totally?
- Do you honor your gut feelings and intuition?
- Do you get indigestion, stomach upsets, heartburn, period pain, bloating?
- Where does fear live in your body? Where does power live in your body?
- Do you know what your wounds sound like? Have you let sound out of the dark, hidden places inside? Do you want to?

- What happened when you first began to bleed as a young woman? Was your period or moon time celebrated? How do you honor your rites of passage now with your daughters, friends? Do you participate in women's circles or ceremonies? Do you want to?
- Do you trust, or compete with, other women?
- Do you maintain any spiritual practices that cultivate energy in your belly?
- Do you breathe rhythmically and deeply? Do you need more energy?
- How much bliss and joy do you allow yourself in your everyday activities?
- Do you have a love for life on Earth?
- What makes you passionate? What inspires you and brings you into the fullness of life?

Other Tools to Heal the Womb

There are many ways to open up the first spiral of the womb, using the physical womb as the vehicle to connect to the emotional. The power of intention, aligned with physical purification, can cleanse and open many layers of the womb; this is a continual process.

Raw foods and juices can help to flush the womb and the whole system. David Wolfe and Queen Afua* are the best people to look to for this. Blessing your water with intention before drinking can also help, as can working with menstrual blood. Members of certain tantric societies used to drink their menstrual blood, boosting estrogen levels and feminine hormones, increasing iron levels, and giving a rush of well-being and vitality. And it is known that pouring nitrogen-rich menstrual blood on plants helps them to grow more.

Along this line, drinking one's own urine also helps to recycle all the vital minerals in the body and helps to flush the system. Drinking

---

*Of particular interest are David Wolfe's *Superfoods: The Food and Medicine of the Future,* and Queen Afua's *Sacred Woman: A Guide to Healing the Feminine Body, Mind, and Spirit.*

urine should not be undertaken until you have been juicing and eating raw foods for a few months. Until your urine is clear, do not drink it.

Opening the womb and yoni to the sunshine, allowing the vital energy of the sun inside you, is greatly vitalizing. Simply find a private space, take off your underwear, and open your legs to the sun, placing your hands on the womb to focus your attention there if needed. Just relax, and breathe in the sun, breathing it into your womb.

Hands-on healing also works with someone you trust enough to allow to place their hands there and send love or Reiki into that area. Magnets can also help when placed over the area. Spend time in nature placing your womb next to the earth, just allowing yourself to embrace and be embraced by Mother Earth. This is so simple, but something we forget to do, and it only takes a few minutes to reconnect. In fact, it is quite enjoyable! The key is to place awareness on the womb rather than the head every day, as this will tune your awareness into that area.

One has to clear the obstacles out of the way to carve more space for the light and life force to reside in your physical womb. As this occurs, your body becomes lighter and more fluid, as your identification is with light rather than matter. Paradoxically, by going more into matter and seeing its restrictions and holding patterns, we spiritualize the body by honoring it. As we honor it for providing us with certain lessons, we begin to identify more with the light and life force inherent in the womb and body.

Certain crystals can help the healing process of the womb. The crystal malachite, the essence of copper, can draw out radiation and absorb energy from painful, diseased, or inflamed areas. Malachite helps restore clearer breathing patterns, releasing and balancing the solar plexus and loosening tension at the diaphragm. It also can clear the womb and energetic pathways of the body, flushing the system with new life flow if taken with the right intention, such as, "Open and clear my womb."

Chrysocolla is one of the best crystals to aid in the healing of feminine reproductive issues and is connected to the feminine masters. Its main attribute is of soft, silent receptivity and the power to be able to rest in this. In addition, the crystals moonstone, pearl, and silver all help to realign oneself back into the feminine lunar path.*

Some Things to Avoid

Never place your laptop computer on your exposed lap, near the womb. Always place a cushion there, or better still, place the laptop on another surface. This radiation can affect the womb and even lead to cancerous growths. Spend less time on the computer and watching TV in general. Do not place your cell phone near the womb, either in a pocket or handbag. Avoid clipping any electrical gadgetry, such as an iPod, near the womb.

Do not take the contraceptive pill. Avoid unprotected sex. Do not insert IUDs into the womb. Avoid slimming patches or tobacco patches and anything chemical like talcum powder or artificial creams or lotions that are placed on the womb. Use natural, organic creams or butters instead. Avoid tampons and instead use moon cups, which are reusable menstrual cups designed by women that hold, rather than absorb or disrupt, one's natural vaginal moisture. Avoid tanning beds!

Perhaps most importantly, honor your womb and yoni by having loving sex and only allowing in a man who loves and honors you. This is a great key to allowing the womb to feel safe, nurtured, respected, and loved, and this will make you bloom. In the next chapter we will explore this topic further.

---

*Use these stones either in solid or liquid form orally, or take baths in them with salts (www.theliquidcrystals.com is a good source for finding these crystals).

2
The Importance of Right Relationships

Keeping Your Boundaries Intact

The womb opens through right relationship. Right relationship is about knowing who your allies are, or who is taking something from you or feeding off your energy in an unhealthy way.

Energies, people, and relationships connect to your womb in ways about which you may have no idea. Old lovers, deceased people, people who wish you no good, all of them can be attached to your womb and drain your energy. If we do not know what, and who, is in our wombs, we cannot have the appropriate boundaries as to what, and who, should be in our wombs.

THE WOMB MANDALA

One of the quickest ways to identify and clear draining patterns, people, and obstacles from the womb is to place your womb in right relationship through the womb mandala. The womb mandala allows us to discover what is actually happening in our womb. It is the first step to becoming aware of whom and what we are feeding, and who and what is feeding us. This mandala works on the four directions by which we orient ourselves in order to live in harmony with the web of life.

To clear out unhealthy relationships, you must move them out of your womb. You must also place all the relationships that you are engaged in into positions that best allow your womb to flourish. It is a delicate balance, but one that your womb needs to have in order to trust and to open.

The Womb Mandala Practice

1. Draw out three wide concentric circles. The first circle has a central point. This central point is *you*.
2. Sit silently and clear your mind. Breathe deeply into your womb. Place your hands on your womb. It is a sphere, a circle. Now visualize yourself in the center of this circle and begin calling in all the people and relationships that your womb is connected to, to make themselves known.

Your Primary Relationships

1. Seeing yourself in this center, look behind you and see who is standing there. Do not allow the mind to dictate or put who you would like to be there. Just be present, open, and curious, and see with your inner eye who is standing directly behind you. Note that this person could be alive or deceased.
2. Then look in front of you, breathe, and feel who is standing there.
3. Continue this and look to your left. Which person is there?
4. Look to your right. Who is standing there?

These are the primary relationships in which your womb is engaged.

Your Secondary Relationships

Now you are going to create a second circle around this primary circle of relationships. Proceed in exactly the same way.

1. Who is behind the person behind you?
2. Who is in front?
3. Who is to the left?
4. Who is to the right?

   This creates a second circle.

Your Most Hidden Relationships

Now proceed exactly in the same way with the third and final circle. This last circle is the periphery. These are the most hidden and seemingly least significant relationships. To create it, simply look around the whole periphery of the second circle and see who is there. Different images and people may float up.

Reading Your Womb Mandala

1. Your mandala will picture you in the center, surrounded by three circles of other beings. You will see three beings in front of you, three behind you, three to your left, and three to your right. It is often surprising to identify the people who are energetically active in our lives.
   - In Front = your guides and teachers
   - Behind = your protectors/supporters/strength
   - To the Right = male power/soul brother/friend or partner
   - To the Left = feminine love/soul sister/friend or wife
2. The first circle of people, those who are closest to you, are those you value the most. They are the most supportive of you and nurturing toward you, and you are nurturing to them in turn. These people are the ones you allow into your deepest and most intimate space.
3. The second circle of people are those you connect to through your womb. They have a strong impact on you and are considered to be "close."
4. The peripheral circle is composed of people whom you trust, although they may not be as close to you as the others. All three

circles represent those people who have the most influence in your life. They are the ones you allow to directly affect you, those whom you have let into your womb and into the deeper aspects of yourself.

5. Take a look again at all the beings in your womb mandala. Do you feel a closeness and warmth with all these beings? Is everyone there in full support of your growth? Do any of these beings deplete your energy?
6. Who do you feel is not in his or her right position? What does this mean for you? For example, if your husband is on your left, in the feminine position, then there is an imbalance in your relationship—he should be on your right. This does not mean that all men should be on your right, but it does make it clear that if you are in intimate relationship with a man, then you are using more of your masculine qualities and he is using more of his feminine ones. If you have a man who is not your partner but a friend or other loved one, this could indicate that he holds a feminine space for you. Similar wisdom holds true for a man who finds a woman on the right side of his womb mandala.
7. If there are people in the mandala who you know do not support you or who you have there out of guilt or obligation, then you have to question this and maybe move them out to the periphery or remove them altogether.
8. Who is it you want in your womb space? This is not about judging anyone, but about discerning where your boundaries are and whom you let into your womb space.

Clearing Negative Energies from Your Womb Mandala

If you have noticed that there are energies present in your womb mandala that do not serve your highest potential, you have to take action. You can take energetic action by cutting cords or commanding with power that these people leave, or you can simply send them love and wish them good-bye. Alternatively, the situation may require you to take direct physical action. You may have to end a relationship or spend less time with an individual. You may need to ask someone for forgiveness, or offer it.

Clearing out old energies is simple:

1. Charge your womb by breath or by intention.
2. Hold the person, place, or situation in mind.
3. Command three times, or more, for them to leave. It is your womb, not theirs.
4. Keep doing the womb mandala practice every morning and evening to facilitate this clearing. Keep checking in with yourself. It eventually takes only a minute or two to do.

As you become centered in your womb awareness, you may find you no longer need to do the practice; it becomes an automatic feeling and knowing. You get to know what is good for your womb, what nourishes and feeds it, what it wishes to share. You also get to know what it does not need, what does not nourish it, and discern what to allow in and what not to allow in.

If you feel you have correct relationships, you will feel supported, nurtured, and nurturing in your daily life. You will have a clearer connection to the web of life and will be more able to manifest your heart's passion and desires in a tangible way.

RELEASING SEXUAL ENERGY FROM THE PAST

All sexual partners from our past have left their energy imprint within the cellular memory of the *yoni* (once again, this term is Sanskrit for "vagina") or *lingam* (Sanskrit for "penis"). It is important to clear old memories, old partners, and past emotions associated with those experiences, for the womb holds memory of every incident that has happened to you and encodings from your ancestors as well. All the emotions, plus the memory of the actual events that triggers those feelings, are stored here.

Once you have made love to a man, his imprint remains in your womb for a maximum of seven years. This means you are carrying him inside you for all this time. The question is, do you want to carry him inside you at all? Carrying someone else's energy inside you after you have separated from them and are in another relationship stops you from fully connecting to the present partner and to the present.

For a promiscuous woman, the buildup of blueprints will actually begin to distort her heart's radiance and ability to engage in true intimacy as so many impressions of others are in the way, blocking the heart's natural outpouring and the womb's comfort. Many promiscuous women often say that they just do not know who they are anymore, that they have become lost to their true joys in life. They have forgotten what excites and ignites them, their purpose is diminished and thinned.

For the man the situation can be as bad. When a man makes love to a woman and releases sperm inside her womb, he becomes attached umbilically to her. A man can become connected to many wombs, which makes his energy cloudy, distorted, and unable to be fully present with just one woman. He becomes lustful, chaotic, and uncontrolled in the worst circumstances. The man has to cut off this connection to many wombs in order to be fully, totally present with just one; otherwise he will always be lusting after someone else.

This can also affect the birth of a baby as the baby will become confused on a subtle level about who its father is. This will of course diminish the bond with the father and create a mutual antagonism. Neither will receive or be able to give the full-blooded love that comes from a clear womb and a clear father-baby relating. Men also become worried by their woman's promiscuous past, questioning whether they are the father of the baby. Confusion and distrust abound.

Healing and clearing the womb before birth allows the best birth to happen for mother and child, giving us hope for future generations of children to be birthed in a clear and conscious way, which will then only benefit society as a whole.

Once these connections are clear, you obtain control of your vital, lusty energy, and you can redirect it to fully serve your full flowering and full empowerment in clarity, integrity, commitment, and wholeness. In dissolving these connections you begin to redirect the energy of *kama,* vital sensual life force, from the womb. This dissolving initiates a signal to the womb that you are ready to open further and deeper. Extra energy releases within you to regenerate and heal from heartbreak and abuses, bringing you deeper peace, fulfillment, and contentment. It also enables you to not make the same mistakes in relationships again! This is all possible when you change the kama energy hidden in the womb in a positive way.

Clearing Womb Attachments

1. Sit comfortably on the floor with the soles of your feet together and your knees spread.
2. Close your eyes, hold your hands over the womb in an inverted triangle, and breathe down into her. Settle down into a quiet space.
3. Visualize one person, preferably an ex-lover, in front of you.
4. See this person as they really are: a mass of shifting colors made of light.
5. See where their cords of connection snake out to connect to you. It could be into the heart, the womb, the solar plexus . . . and so on.
6. As you see these cords clearly, focus on one. Feel its connection to you, and any pictures, sensations, or memories connected to it.
7. Focus all your energy onto this cord, all your attention. Take a deep breath into your womb.
8. With all your might, and with your breath, raise up your hands, and cut the cord with a mighty exhale of breath.
9. Do this three times. Notice your feelings.
10. Once you have done this and taken note of your feelings, ask yourself, "What did I learn from this situation in a positive way? Did it teach me compassion, discernment, wisdom, love?"

Do not rush through this process. Doing it once properly can dissipate many charges if you sit and take your time. After all, this is your life! If you do this well, you will notice the benefit and the release of much stuck emotional energy. You will not need to do it more than once if you do it properly the first time, with full focus.

As you clear out your womb you become more aware of what is lurking in there. You might be hanging on to someone deceased, or to old lovers, or to people trying to drain your energy. Or you could be too attached to an experience, person, or environment that is toxic for you. In this exploration you can become more aware of your connection to the whole web of life. As this connection deepens, more stored memories surface. You may choose to do womb mandalas every week as well as in new situations in which you find yourself. Notice the changes that occur.

CLEARING THE HEART ARC LINE

Within the auric field, both men and women have a potent ring of energy that is located from the center of the ear, up and over the crown, and into the other ear. This is known as an Arc Line. We see this depicted as halos in angelic or religious art. This Arc Line is our antenna and a highly attuned piece of the subtle sensory system. We can detect danger, negativity, and hidden agendas within moments of being within a disturbed field.

A woman has a second Arc Line, which is between each nipple, arcing over her heart. This second Arc Line carries the blueprint of every lover she has ever had on a heart level. The moment a woman exchanges juices, whether this is kissing, oral intimacy, or full-bodied intercourse, a snap shot or photograph of this person's essence is embedded within her Arc Line.

When I was told about the second Arc Line, I knew instantly I was being told Truth. I had been a very adventurous woman, and the sexual arena was my old playground. I made it my business to study and directly experience this second Arc Line, and of course clear it as swiftly as possible. Through meditation and Jyana yoga (yoga of self-inquiry), all women can clear their Arc Lines and enter into a relationship free, authentic, and fresh, with no reference points to the past, or to ex-lovers. Every man and woman can sense a third person, a ghost from the past. Clear yourself, and show others how to do the same. (A. A.)

Clearing Out the Arc Line

1. Sit in a comfortable position, with your spine straight and neck lengthened.
2. Begin to feel and sense this halo of light between each nipple arcing over your heart. You can trace it with your fingers if you want to.
3. Moving through your timeline, either present to past or past to present, begin to visualize and sense all those with whom you have "exchanged juices."
4. Place your hands in Gyan Mudra (first finger and thumb pad touching) as you recall a memory or impression or past lovers.
5. Inhale through your nostrils as you comb your hand through the Arc Line; exhale as you pull the line out way beyond your chest.
6. Continue to do this for eleven minutes, which is enough time to stir and clear the emotional body.

Do both the Womb Clearing and the Heart Arc Line practice every day until you feel clear and free from the past. Both practices working together on womb and heart with clear intention will swiftly bring up anything residing in both womb and heart, and then clear it. Remember, it is natural to feel emotions such as pain, loss, and grief during this process, which is deep and vast for a woman. Be kind to yourself.

I was shocked when I saw and felt the evidence as my pen drew the inner map of all that I was holding within my womb essence. I saw the foundation upon which I was coming from, in many senses of the word!

I drew a shadow man that had haunted me throughout my childhood in feverish dreams, I drew the forceps and metallic instruments that brought me into this world, I saw the bloodied sheets and harsh confines of the hospital that housed me and the greatest insight: I was alone, there was no one there. There was not one person or archetype that I was receiving support or guidance from. It was a bleak and barren place. All that I had ever known, and all that I was, dissolved in that moment. Here within my womb lying untouched, unhealed, and very stark was the ground that I stood upon.

All that can be done in a moment like that is drop down into it and face it head on, or rather the truth of the matter, heart on. So I began work to remove those energetic imprints and reintroduce new ones that supported and strengthened my integrity as a woman. I began working with the mandala day and night until I could tune in within seconds and see the whole picture. Now it's second nature, I can sense the mandala in every moment, and the important process of clearing at the end of the day.

Now, my womb is ready and more than willing to take on any situation that may arise. As far as my sexuality is concerned, I felt with a clear womb that I could allow the man into the deeper parts of myself. I felt undefended, unprotected, and dare I say it, "virginal." (A. A.)

As I entered my womb space I had various people in the wrong places. It was like my womb was gender confused. This made complete sense to me. Although happily heterosexual, I had received more fathering than mothering as a child, and so my womb space contained a lot of masculine energy. Also, there seemed to be a very strong tie with my father that no longer served me as a middle-aged woman, and I was able to reorganize the energy of this space to be more soft and feminine.

I now feel I have for the first time in my life more feminine support. I can see the people in my mandala and really feel them. I can trust who supports me, and it is a very new and reassuring feeling. I had spent years blocking the feminine and disowning it as weak and vulnerable and yet since embracing this vulnerability and femininity I have found my true power. The womb is a place I now go on a daily basis to check in with how I'm feeling mentally, emotionally, and spiritually. It is like an oracle universe has opened up in my awareness and all the answers I've ever wanted to know are right here inside me. (S. F.)

BALANCING THE MASCULINE AND FEMININE ASPECTS OF SELF

> *When we empower ourselves as the feminine we empower the masculine at the same time. We cannot belittle the masculine without belittling the feminine in us first.*
>
> JIVAN

Women have the power to create, but they cannot do it alone. When the woman has healed her womb it naturally opens to embrace and include the masculine. In this union, the woman brings the man into this sanctuary and guides the masculine to act upon the creation of love. In no way is the man left out; on the contrary, the womb draws the masculine unto itself, and together they unite in this crucible of love where all can be healed and birthed.

When a woman is in the first level of the spiral of healing the womb, she may become confused between the masculine and feminine aspects of self. This can result in a general lack of grounding and alignment on all levels of self, lowered life force, and a loss of earth connection. When the womb is ungrounded, we can be scattered, inefficient, moody, and exhausted. It can seem like we never have enough time to get what we want done, and the things we want always seem just out of reach. We can be reactive, unable to step back from people, events, and relationship experiences to allow appropriate action. We feel that life is too fast, that it is passing by too quickly, and we cannot quite catch up to it.

A woman's sense of confusion about the masculine and feminine aspects of self, however, may also lead to an increased masculine drive based on fear, the need to prove oneself, and the adoption of values needed to survive in a man's world. All excess masculine behavior is based on fear or pain, wounds that need to be seen and felt.

Disconnection to the true feminine manifests with tightness at the heart-womb, blocking the giving and receiving of love. Living life in an emotional state, repressing, fearing true feeling, makes us ignorant of life's larger cycles. The fear of working with the essential wisdom of polarities and the disavowment of the dark or shadow aspects leads to disempowerment. Power is found in the darkness once you are brave enough to consistently venture into it and reclaim your power. In this wisdom you acquire the willpower to transform and empower self.

You know that deep within you there is so much more, so much more you deserve and that you have felt. But you have forgotten about it and relegated it to a dream, a fantasy, a romantic illusion. And now you have settled for "comfort" and pleasantry—and left out part of your soul in this deal, this bargain. At any time you can notice this thread, as a whispered thought, an unusual feeling, a hope, a dream, a chance meeting, a stumbling across this book perhaps . . . and a longing in the heart. Follow it, act upon it, do something radical, and enjoy the bliss, and adventure, of this path.

Move for the best; for you deserve it and can attain it. It is waiting for you patiently, for you to notice it, follow it, and act upon it.

THE NEVER-ENDING SPIRAL

As you bring more life force and light into your awareness and womb, remember that you are on a spiral path. With each turn of the ascending spiral, there can be an equal turn on the descending spiral. This is a continual process, so the more we evolve the more we have to tune in to and use these clearing ways to keep us in harmony. This is a spatial process that is always happening. Every evolutionary spurt we go through is a gateway to hold and embody more light in our physical forms.

As more light comes in, more darkness can arise. As we clear the womb to open up more space for our souls to emerge, we release the burdens and density of the physical world. The womb here is an earth-centered love, a physical nurturing and opening that attracts all fear to itself that is stuck on the physical and emotional level and dissolves it. As we start to clear these obstacles, commitment and dedication to our healing arises: we are ready to do whatever it takes to grow and shed these limiting beliefs. Even if we think we are beyond certain healings, we reenter them in order to fully embody our highest potential on a different turn of the spiral.

THE COMMITMENT

From this moment on, or at least for the remainder of this book, a commitment needs to be made.

- A commitment to only partake in authentic love making
- A commitment to never allow yourself to be entered by a man unless it is in honor, giving, respect, integrity, and love.
- A commitment to "make love," not have sex, not to follow lust, not to be goal orientated, that is, chasing an orgasm or a temporary fix to a problem.
- A commitment to not compromise yourself in any way. Do not partake in any sexual behavior that is not holding your highest potential. Explain gracefully without partaking, as this is the first step toward becoming the authentic, elegant, and empowered woman you truly are.

Place the whole of you behind these vows, and stand for what you know to be true.

PART TWO

The Second Spiral

3
The Flowering Womb

Sensing from the Heart of the Womb

The second spiral is called the Flowering Womb. This is felt when the womb itself blooms through your attention and conscious focus on it, and it begins to open. This opening occurs as you drop your center of gravity and focus down from your head into the womb, so your center of power, awareness, and action emanates from here.

During times of crisis or transition, individual or collective, we are forced to look beyond everyday life for answers—to look internally, where the answers lie. In this action we have a deep knowing about something else that lies beyond the world of appearances, divisions, and conflict. This something else is the voice, pulse, and flow of the womb.

THE VOICE OF THE WOMB

As your actions and focus start to come from the womb, you start to dialogue with, and listen to, the womb's voice. The voice of the womb is a voice long forgotten, but once contacted it becomes a staunch ally and your inner guru. This is more than the voice of your intuition; this is the voice of your feminine essence, where you birth and create from, the center of your unique power as a woman.

The womb becomes your most trusted friend, a guide to listen to and to ask your deepest questions of. Many women have shared with me that once they recognize this voice and wisdom of their womb, they realize that what they once thought was the voice of their spirit guides, Spirit, or even God was actually the voice of their womb! They had been placing this voice outside, when in fact it has always been within.

The Sounds of the Womb

The earth is pregnant with heaven, which is immortality.

The sounds of the womb activate the womb. By using certain sounds and sounding them from the womb space, we can resonate and feel the depths and richness of our own center. The sounds of the womb focus on exploring your individual messages of power that spring from your center. This form of deep, primal chanting can express that which may seem inexpressible, that which you have felt deep within but have not been able to articulate, voice, or give sound to. These universal, primal sounds help to unlock wisdom we have not allowed ourselves to know, or have been too scared to let ourselves approach.

Sound creates life, and life is born from sound. By sounding the womb, from where all life arises and passes away back into, we can begin to enter this space of birthing and dying.

The Sound of *AH*—Opening to Create

AH is the first sound of creating, the opening of the creative flow of life. It is one of the first sounds of orgasm, the sound of pleasure and bliss. *AH!* It releases, unlocks, and opens yourself to the highest potential and is a sound that is present in all life. If you simply stop and rest for a moment, you can hear the sound of *AH* in nature, in your body, and all around you. Many cultures use this meditation to tune in to the sound behind all life, and by using this sound you too can relax into a deeper state of consciousness.

The Sound of *OH*—Opening the Womb

OH is the sound that gives life to connection, to relationship. It breathes in life force into the web of life, energizing and expanding, constantly moving. In its constant unbroken movement, *OH* constantly renews itself in each moment.

OH is the sound of the original womb, the sound that occurs with birth. It is one of the main sounds of orgasm. "Oh, oh, oh!" as when a woman is being penetrated, and the womb is truly touched and felt; this is the sound that naturally arises in all women regardless of race or country. *OH* dominates words meaning either the whole or a void, such as womb, dome, hole.

The Sound of *AI*—The Sound of Creating

AI is *I AM*, the soul identity. It links the individual self with the larger Self. *AI* is the sound that dissolves all pain and suffering, for suffering becomes joy as we embrace our own self. *AI* is the start of the final process of manifestation, where we sing our song of creating—our soul song. In India it is the sound of Saraswati, the goddess of music and creativity.

The Sound of *AU*—The Love of Creating

AU is made from *AH* and *U*. Together they create the first sound of love in manifestation, where man and woman merge in order to create and manifest. This singing forth into creation is a great wave of bliss. *AI AU* is the first movement of the formless into form—it is the descent of light and ideas into form and manifestation.

The Sound of *OM MA AUM*—The Hum of the Universe

OM is the background sound vibration or "hum" of the universe. It is the first sound of creating, used to attune us to the sound that underlies all life.

MA is the sound of the mother found in all languages. It is one of the first sounds a baby makes and is the sound that most of us relate to when we call out for help, for love, for comfort. *MA* is the sound of the heart yearning, calling out to the universe, the most common sound found in all cultures, which we all instinctively identify with.

MA loves us all, no matter what we do and who we are. It can only love and support, for that is its very nature—it cannot do anything else. Together the mantra *AUM MA OM* swirling deep inside the womb evokes the mother of love resonating with the sound behind creation, the basis of all creativity.

Sounding Out the Womb

What do you wish to birth, and what do you wish to have pass away from your life?

1. With the above intention/question in mind, sound into your womb. Choose your own combinations of sounds, the ones that feel right to you, that speak to you, that resonate with your belly.
2. Place your hands over your womb, and take a few deep breaths to center your attention there. Drop down from your mind, and rest for a moment.
3. Focus on one intention. Now drop this gently into the womb, and sound whatever sounds feel right for you.

The Second Womb Dialogue

Moving through the second spiral, you learn to discern the collective limiting beliefs and acquired defense structures within the feminine collective consciousness. The means of getting what you want through manipulating men, aligned with the acknowledging of your essentially open, inviting, and vulnerable nature, built in part on women's physical difference from men, allows deeper healing and empowerment to occur.

It is here that we begin to exercise self-authority and create real boundaries. This also entails the expression of one's inner world and externalizing it to others. Self-empowerment is an action. Just by speaking it, you will become empowered, and evolve.

Ask your womb the following questions. You might be surprised by the answers.

- Do you exercise authority in your life and with people?
- Do you have clear boundaries in your relationships?
- Are you overly attached to anyone or anything?
- Are you honest with yourself and your partner? Are you prepared to be radically honest with yourself and all those you are close to?
- Do you appreciate life and those around you? Do you feel appreciated?
- Do you compete with any other woman at any time? Do you give your power, knowing, authority away to any man at all?
- Do you sexually manipulate men in any way? Do you, or have you, used men?
- Do you commune with any woman in a nonverbal way? Do you engage in women's circles and sharings? Do you share deep inquiry time with women? Do you collectively sit down and share what you are feeling?
- Do you take a lot of things personally in your life?
- Do you need affirmation from others? Do you care too much what others think? Are you attached to what people *may* say, think, or feel about you?
- Are you scared of speaking in public?
- Do you have memories of being persecuted? Do you feel a lot of shame and guilt?
- Do you want to be a pioneer, or a victim? Do you feel it is someone else's fault?
- Do you trust in life and feel supported by the universe? Do you trust that right now you are learning exactly what you need to?
- Do you have the energy to move forward? Do you feel stuck in an area you cannot put your finger on? Do you have nagging or repeating intuitions and feelings that you do not act on?
- Do you know you are truly responsible for all of your feelings?
- Do you know you are co-creating everything that is happening to you?
- Can you see your emotions, and not be run by them?

I have a new voice . . . it's that soft feminine knowing voice that I used to reject and ignore. It's my mother's wisdom, it's her essence and her lovely subtle offerings of advice that she allows me to choose, if I so wish, to heed or ignore. It's my voice and choice.

Before I heard that soft wisdom, I really didn't know I had a choice. Eternally grateful for that feminine whisper, for it is that whisper which has become louder and clearer on the inside than the ones shouting no *on the outside, and I feel for once that I have mastered my life. As I surrender more into this state of allowing and knowingness there is another feminine voice emerging. It is an oracle of truth, it's even softer and more nurturing than my mother could ever be, it is the voice of my womb, the real authentic me, and as I get to know her, I feel more in tune with life itself. I can relax in the joy of life and follow the desires that make me smile, laugh, and have fun again. I can play, I can laugh, I can commune with nature and do the craziest things that are perfectly all right to do in love and laughter. Now I'm really living and loving. (S. F.)*

Womb Breathing

Womb breathing can help clarify the questions you are asking your womb and get deeper answers. Womb breathing begins to bring attention, breath, and light into the womb, energizing her, cleansing her, and focusing her. This also works with men and their *haras* (seats of internal energies, much as wombs are for women). Womb breathing requires patience and gentle presence from you, as it is done in a sacred manner with the clear intention to heal, soothe, and open the gateway into the womb.

To begin, find a place and time where you will be undisturbed and feel safe to make sound or rest in the silence. Be with this breath, and give it your undivided attention and focus. Feelings and emotions may begin to surface, so be in your allowing, open, receptive, feminine nature, and go wherever the practice takes you. Most of all, enjoy! This can be a pleasurable, sensual experience.

1. Lie on your back with feet on the floor and knees bent, as if you were giving birth.

2. Make yourself comfortable with cushions to support your head.
3. Place both hands over the womb and make conscious connection with yourself, your womb, and your breath.
4. Begin to bring your focus to your PC muscles (the area between your vagina and anus).
5. Take your time to find these muscles, and then contract them.
6. On a slow rhythmic inhale, squeeze the PC muscles together and suck the breath into the womb. Feel and see the breath as light coming into the womb.
7. Treat the breath with a quality of preciousness. Imagine light flowing into the womb.
8. Hold the breath in the womb, while squeezing the PC muscles, (as if you were holding in from urinating), and with your hands make slow large circles, clockwise and counterclockwise.
9. As you make circles, feel the light of the breath bathing and suffusing the whole womb.
10. On the exhale, relax the PC muscles, pushing the breath through the PC.
11. As you release the breath, feel the subtlety of the light flowing *out* of the yoni.
12. Feel as if you are making love with yourself and cleansing your womb with golden light.
13. And then again inhale, pulling in the PC, holding the breath in the womb, making circles with your hands.
14. Repeat this for 10 minutes.

How do you feel?

THE PULSE OF THE WOMB

We start to connect into the second spiral by feeling the pulse of life force directly into the womb itself. Just as you have a heartbeat, so do you have a womb beat, the heartbeat of birthing. Each is incomplete without the other, and each needs the other in order for you to become a whole woman, uniting love and power in your body. As both pulse beats unite, a dynamic, joyful, orgasmic, life-affirming *yes!* flows through you.

Feeling the pulse of the womb allows that which you have been holding onto to release out of your system, as the pulse brings to life that which has been stagnant and buried. This pulse is a direct reconnection to your core, clearing negative electrical charges, memories, traumas, and shocks of the past. It is unique to any other form of energy or bodywork.

In the past the pulse was known as the dragon energy, the primordial serpent power, raw untamed feminine energy, wild and free. The womb contains this in the form of a strong ball of energy, a concentrated nucleus of living, fertile, vibrant aliveness and sensual power that once released floods the whole system with its life flow.

I noticed one morning during meditation how my womb was involuntarily pulsing, with a beat as regular as my heart. I was not sexually aroused, nor particularly energized, yet this mysterious womb-beat begged for further investigation. The more I concentrated on it, the deeper it became. Even when I tried to control or stop it, its beat persisted.

This was incredible! From a woman's perspective, it was as if my womb were calling out to my man, the pulse a cry for connection. Not as a mortal woman wanting her man, no, more like the earth praying for heaven. As I pulsed, I began to draw Padma's subtle light up into my womb, heart, and brain. His light was everywhere, and I was literally blinded. As I closed my eyes, all I could see was white light. This wave of the most exquisite form of love was moving way beyond my body, out into my auric field, and radiating out into the space of consciousness. (A. A.)

For most it is not possible to pass alone through this strong, deep, energy, to welcome it, to make love with it. You can't give birth without being in connection. You can't give birth in a state of seclusion, for to give birth means we stay completely in connection with All That Is, with the pain and the death, with the purest joy and love, with it all. When we welcome it, love it, and make love with all parts of being, then a great magic can come true. You can give birth to the mystery of life. (U. W.)

Only the connection between the womb and the heart can make this ancient primordial power really live again.

Allowing the pulse to activate and charge through us makes us fluid, able to flow with what is happening without being fixed to a story or belief. The charges dissolve, and blissful joy explodes within us, flooding and connecting our whole being, dissolving anything that is not this. This is a potent experience and really brings us home to the power of the womb and the joy contained within it.

The Tibetan Pulsing Practice

This is a practice to begin to access the pulse of the womb. It comes from the Tibetan tradition and has been used for thousands of years by Tibetan monks to open and clear their bodymind system. It is used to spectacular effect when done properly, releasing the binds of the womb and allowing the free flow of life force to rush through the body. It is best done in a guided context in a safe retreat setting, but I have included it here so you can get a taste of it.

Pulsing is done with two partners of the same weight and can be done with men and women.

1. Put on some sensual, percussive music that you feel you can move to. Partner A lies on the ground. Partner B straddles partner A, sitting gently on the womb area, placing the knees on the ground on either side of Partner A's hips.
2. Make sure you are both comfortable. Talk to each other to ensure you are sitting on the womb.
3. Sit and meditate for a moment, tuning in to each others energy and feelings. Breathe in harmony with your partner. Inhale and exhale at the same time.
4. When ready, Partner B gently starts to rock his or her pelvis back and forth on the womb of partner A, generating life force energy.
5. After a few minutes, increase the tempo of the pulsing. Sensations and feelings will arise; simply breathe into them.

6. At the end of about fifteen minutes, relax. Now swap positions, and repeat.
7. Each time you do the pulsing, both partners benefit from it.

A Prayer to the Womb

Beloved Womb of Mine, be my redeemer, my internal teacher, my divine physician.

Thank you for your presence in my life.

I surrender to you all that I am, all that I think, all that I feel, and all that I have. I recognize in this moment that yours is the power to heal and make me whole.

You who have the power to work miracles, you who rule time and space, please take me deep within and hold me there forevermore.

THE FLOW OF THE WOMB

The second spiral exists in our bodies, and the larger Gaian body, through flow. In flow, we become fluid, assuming any shape as required in order to communicate. This contrasts with our waking state of consciousness, where we are dependent on the five senses to translate our experience of the world into meaningful information.

Flow arises from the release of the pulse of the womb and body. Flow is the process of completing naturally, miraculously, and easily an action that we usually find to be difficult, or impossible. Flow is being in a state of effortless consciousness, where instead of trying to do something or force our achievements, we just allow it to happen. Having this experience of relaxed allowing, of graceful simple ease, shows us what our potential is, and once we are aware of this potential, it can grow and flow more.

When we flow, thinking becomes an expression of ever-flowing movement, a fluid understanding that can be accessed anytime and applied into any situation. Like water, fluid thought envelops objects from all sides.

Only when thinking dwells on a particular content, a particular form, does it order itself to create an idea, for every idea, every organic form, arises in a process of flow, until the movement congeals into a form. If we follow nature's vibrational, flowing patterns, we act in this fluid manner, able to be whatever is needed, any facet of consciousness, in any moment.

In the second spiral, knowing is applied from the womb in a fluid, instant, synchronous way in any situation. The mind is not required as the womb acts in the moment. The womb blooms when the heart opens, embraces, and is embraced, touches, and is touched. When the heart opens, the womb softens and flowers. These two powerhouses, when united, give and receive without measure, interchanging when required, so that your body literally begins to breathe itself.

> *When you are joyous, look deep into your heart and you shall find it is only that which has given you sorrow that is giving you joy. When you are sorrowful, look again into you heart, and you shall see that in truth you are weeping for that which leads to your delight. (A. A.)*

When we truly touch something, and are touched, all barriers between us and others dissolve. A deeper understanding, softness, depth of knowing arises, but in the sovereignty of freedom, wild and free, owned by no one, and owning nothing in its free flow. It is a sensual, holy, sacred feeling—a feeling you can bow to and make love with at the same time; it is an intimate, open, spontaneous meeting in another as complementary and as equal to you in all ways.

It is only through unconditional love that such a life can come to be born. In the second and third spirals, we discover commitment in relationships rather than attachment. Such a being supports, accepts, and holds, like the Grail or the Chalice, all the power and wild force of the feminine throughout the ages in love, supporting her in transparency. This man has to be nobody, yet everybody—space-like and loving, both personally and impersonally.

To open the womb requires this totality. Nothing less will do. All that you have ever learned and relied upon within the realm of relationships has to go. Only innocence and a childlike wonder hold the keys to this path. Whatever you think you may know about love, sexuality, and relating has to put aside, along with all your weaponry, ways and tactics to stay safe, and most importantly your past experiences and lovers.

In esoteric traditions in the past, the woman held energy silently, as a Grail, crucible, or womb—a container for energy. Then the man would express it, use it, take it outward from the crucible, bringing it into form. Similarly, men can hold the space for women to express; men can act as the Grail, too, where the woman brings creation into form.

In both cases, one was the lover or the loved; one was more powerful, more in control than the other. The two met in this distorted equilibrium, where a weak man was with a strong woman, and a weak woman with a strong man. Even in their separation, down throughout the ages, man and woman have mirrored this fear to one another. The fear of not being whole, and free, and needing the other to make them whole.

Now the tide is turning. As man and woman come together equally, the One that forms in the union of He and She can be used by either form, slipping into each form as and when it suits them. In this primal cauldron we can transmute and transform the deepest darkest energies of the psyche, refining the dross, the shadow of our selves, into gold.

For when we become intimate and truly open, when we use the sexual energy and the deep, deep emotions that come with it, we cannot hide or disguise any part of ourselves. We become naked, literally, and exposed. We learn to experience everything in order to be in harmony with everything. There are no attachments or aversions, simply acceptance, and beyond that, joy.

Each tear of pain shed is one tear closer to the end of this cycle of separation. And this cycle of tears stops when we realize that this whole world, all our relationships, all our reflections, is all us. It stops when we see the divine in everyone's eyes, from Hitler to Christ. For we have all experienced moments of being both a Hitler and a Christ at different times on the Wheel of Life.

4
The Power of the Womb

Dying into the Vortex of the Womb

The womb is the holder and repository of the creative force of instinctual sexuality, the flow of vital dynamic life force, or Shakti, with love. When a woman brings together this instinctual nature with an awareness of the divine within herself, her full creative potential becomes expressed.

This sacred nature is expressed through love and magnified in her relationships with others and the natural world. She lives it through her sexuality, her attunement to the rhythms and cycles of nature, and through birthing. She honors this through her body and her unique ways of expressing herself, knowing who she is, and simply being this. By simply being herself she unites her instinctual nature, the creation, the earth, and matter with the power of consciousness, transforming them all in her daily life.

THE PRIMAL FORCE OF THE WOMB

Deep within all of you lays this primal power, an unstoppable primal force. Chaotic and uncontrollable, teeming with life and overflowing passion, this power hides in the darkness, the mystery of creation between form and formless. It is from here that all life pours in an inexhaustible torrent.

This force can be as scary and as threatening as it is loving and nurturing. If you have resistance then you will experience chaos and fear. If you have no resistance then you will experience its bliss and be taken on a roller-coaster ride that makes no sense to the mind, but enlivens and screams life to all your senses and soul.

When we encounter such power, most people respond to it in fear, the fear that it will have power, and control, over them. Fearing it will destroy them. And it will! It will destroy the resistance to being this power; it will wipe out part of who you think you are, the greatest fear of all. It threatens your very identity, who you treasure yourself to be as an individual; it cares not for these boundaries, blasting through them, taking you to the beginnings of creation, before form, before thought, before gender. It is freedom, spontaneous, wild and free, and has no order, structure, or reason to it.

It is the fertile, fecund darkness, the depths of our instinctual, gut-driven nature and intuition. When we cut off from it, it consumes us, making us greed- and lust-driven for a satisfaction that we know we possess but do not know how to tap in to except through outer means.

Denying the feminine denies a vital part of our aliveness, our connection to the web of life, to eating life itself. Denying the primal leads us to overindulge in the external, instead of living what lies within us; it leads us to destroying and devouring ourselves, creating a wasteland, a desert of consciousness instead of a rich, lush forest of fertile abundance. When we allow the dark feminine to take us, pull us, possess us, we live in wild freedom, wild joy, unpredictable moment to moment, loving this unpredictability as our true nature. Raw power refines into bliss.

The moment I became aware of this power, I knew it was alive within me. She guided me to my darkest rivers and stood by me as I roared with creation. She had my back, as I too wandered the desert, barren and torn with this world, and she was there as I stood without hope, at

> *the meaninglessness of life. I knew I was the erupting volcano and the tender sweet embrace embalmed as one. With that realization, all that can ever be done is to accept the vastness of the spectrum that woman is. (A.A.)*

To share our sexuality without shame is natural. There are no taboos, no conventions of "polite society" to adhere to, as there are no rules in the feminine—just flow. This flow appears to be chaos to the mind that lies stuck and in resistance to the flow of life, afraid of the unknown Self that lies so vast beyond what the mind can ever try to understand. The energy or catharsis created by the mind's resistance has no form or rhyme to it, so it gets called chaos. Yet all flow is the experience of the life force in its essence.

Chaos and powerlessness of the ego, disorientation and helplessness of the mind are what the conditioned mind encounters when confronted by this energy. In the exhaustion and the giving up of the mind, the giving up of resistance to the flow, one relaxes and flows into the most creative force in the earth, releasing the mind into a seething ocean of infinite possibilities where anything becomes possible.

This is deep, deep nourishment—nourishment before words, ideas, and even emotions. It shows you how the world is fed and works; it shows you how women throughout the ages have tapped in to the power that creates new realities.

The unformed, uncontrolled, seething life force lies behind all appearances, all structures, all apparently ordered and reasonable things we do. It is always there as the substrata of life, waiting for us to tap in to and break the rigidities of what we have self-created in order to live what true creating is, moment by naked, vital, pulsing moment. All philosophy, ideas, spiritual systems . . . most of it is trying to hide away from this force, trying to rationalize, spiritualize, and politically correct our most natural of impulses.

We are led to love through this fertile uninhibited force, dissolving the ideas, beliefs, and thoughts that stand in the way of the pulsing life force of wild joy, the expression of love that is untrammeled by convention. It says yes to love and in its heart connects all life-forms through love once you penetrate into its mysteries and have allowed it to flow through you unchecked, once you have allowed it to take you without reservation.

It leads to the softness, the gentling of love; the peace that passes all understanding communing with the wild freedom that joy creates. This a radical force for change, for liberation, for entrance into oneness and freedom without boundaries, without rules, without ideas, just the pulsing, vital flow of living love itself. Surrendering to this primal life allows you to experience the love that creates all life. And this is vital for women, and men, to reclaim.

This primordial passion becomes nonpersonal; it stops having an object for its desire and is just free desire, desire that runs freely throughout the body, womb, and heart; energy without barriers. This desire is pure joy and sexuality raised into the power of fertile attraction, loving radiation, and carefree abundance.

The womb speaks the language of love. Nothing else will nurture and nourish her and provide her the safety she needs to flower. The womb can open and receive its nourishment if it is showered into her palpably. She knows love intimately and deeply in all its many facets and flavors.

THE BIRTHING OF LIFE AND TRUE KNOWLEDGE

The womb is first awakened by bringing to her the gifts of presence, devotion, deep respect, appreciation, and the feeling qualities of love and adoration. This begins the birthing phase. The womb will then begin to speak of her needs and desires.

The womb does not understand the intellect and the ways of the world. She does not hear or respond to the voice of fear and judgment. She will not expose herself to the impure, and she will not trust to bare her fruit for the foolish and ignorant. One must be prepared to take great risks, rise to challenges, and be tested in unexpected ways.

The jewel of an open womb is not for the meek and halfhearted. It is for the brave, the courageous and strong-willed. It is the loving, open, and receptive soul that can allow constant penetration of a powerful transformational love that is beyond comprehension. For her to reveal herself she needs to feel a genuine commitment, passionate loyalty, and a love that surpasses all worldly desires.

When one dies into womb, true knowledge and life is birthed. One must lose everything it thinks it needs in order to gain everything the heart truly desires. The womb's only needs and desires are to feel the warmth of love and support from the feminine and masculine. Both male and female qualities are necessary for her to open and expand. The womb yearns to attune to the masculine, to feel his strength, power, protection, passion, and love. The feminine must inhabit the womb, in all its innocence and power, and the masculine must submit to her wisdom and guidance.

All separate desires and individual agendas must be surrendered to the wisdom the womb holds. Total respect and humility is offered for this voice to come forth. This voice is recognizable as a soft, powerful clarity, distinguished by its unwavering nature to create the good, the holy, and the beautiful. It is the voice of the feminine, pure, gentle, and graceful yet powerful, direct, and deep. It does not compromise or search for approval. It does not speak of duality nor does it muster words of fear and doubt. It remains calm and precise and knows exactly what is required in each and every moment.

There is a need for vigilance and discernment. The way to distinguish truth from illusion, the voice of ego from the voice of the womb, is by the quality of its tone. The ego is hurried and familiar and will cause disturbance to the flow of breath. It will talk in an unrefined harshness that will try to argue, defend, project, belittle, attack, or manipulate. This language is foreign to the true reality of our being. The womb will soothe, invite, inspire, and will, more often than not, be very surprising. It has no past or future, no reference point to anything outside the present.

The womb has to become the master, for it is the creator and the voice of divine wisdom. This authority grows, its conviction and guidance deepens, when it is respected and acted upon without delay, doubt, or hesitation.

THE VITALITY OF THE OPEN WOMB

The *wombgasm* occurs when the womb itself starts to experience deep, distinct orgasmic pulses, bursts, or waves, different from vaginal or even full-body orgasms. When the womb receives consistent attention, nurturance, and unconditional love, the womb starts to stir, flower, and come alive, beginning to attune to its vastness and its energetic subtleties. If the woman is diligently attentive to its presence, new and amazingly unique sensations can be experienced.

The womb becomes a portal of wisdom and will, highly sensitive, acquiring a life and voice uniquely its own, separate from the mind, with its own unerring wisdom and such a distinct, clear voice that it is impossible to ignore. In following this voice, a woman may initiate shifts, feeling guided into changing her spirituality along with her lifestyle, her diet, and those relationships that do not serve its flowering and further unfolding.

The womb becomes exquisitely sensitive to tastes, feelings, thoughts, and sensations and can respond to loving touch with openness, delight, and deep pleasure. This pleasurable feeling can literally be felt in the womb as tremendous bliss and miraculous joy. Explosions or bursts of palpable loving energy spontaneously erupt, felt as orgasms in the womb itself. This orgasmic feeling is rich and divine in essence and can bring a woman to extraordinary depths and heights of love. It is truly a blessing and a miraculous gift for a woman to feel this mysteriously awesome, beautifully divine sensation occurring in her womb.

Imagine a Woman

Imagine a woman who believes it is right and good that she is a woman
A woman who honors her experience and tells her stories
Who refuses to carry the sins of others within her body and life

Imagine a woman who believes she is good
A woman who trusts and respects herself
Who listens to her needs and desires and meets them with tenderness and grace

Imagine a woman who has acknowledged the past's influence in the present
A woman who has walked through her past
Who has healed the present

Imagine a woman who authors her own life
A woman who exerts, initiates, and moves on her own behalf
Who refuses to surrender except to her truest self and wisest voice

Imagine a woman who imagines the divine in her image and likeness

Imagine a woman in love with her own body
A woman who believes her own body is enough, just as it is
Who celebrates her body as an exquisite resource

Imagine a woman who honors the face of the goddess
A woman who celebrates the accumulation of her years and her wisdom
Who refuses to use precious energy disguising the changes in her body and life

Imagine a woman who values the women in her life
A woman who sits with others
Who is reminded of the truth about herself whenever she forgets

Now imagine yourself as this woman . . .

Patricia Lynn Reilly

BREAKTHROUGH

As the pulse of the womb releases, we generate energy, power, and strength. Grit and determination allied with exuberance lead to your breakthrough, giving you the power to break down old patterns that keep your energy from flowing and from manifesting new visions that reflect your heart's desire. Here we find the dense irrational chaos that is danger, that is radical, that is the essence of risk itself. Without facing this danger, without going to the edge of your experience and beyond, you can never become who you truly are. You have to dive in to the deep unknown to know who you are.

I remember being with a spiritual teacher who asked me, was I a person who practiced something, and was that practice the foundation upon which I was built? My cover was blown in that instant. I knew in that moment that the meek answer was yes, I was that person. All that I had become, the empire I had created around me, had to fall. I took a radical step as I decided to let everything go. I stopped my practice, I let my teaching name go. I dissolved my teaching "schedule," and within days an uneasy, nagging, knowing voice began to eat away at me.

I was becoming no one special, with nothing going on. This revelation brought with it tremendous heat, sweats, nausea, fear, feelings of failure, and eventually a huge death. I was birthed into simply being a woman, nameless, ageless, pigeonhole-less, free and whole . . . and no one, and yet of course, everyone. It takes a certain courage to face this death and an unmoving trust in the process. (A. A.)

The new vision that births through you from this is focused, directed, yet expansive. It encompasses and embraces many possibilities, never losing sight of where it wishes to go and how it is going to birth. By opening up to all possibilities, while remaining grounded, centered, and in your power, you can birth.

When you open to all things, then all things can pour through you. As this occurs, you expand, and the greatest healings occur, as you are now embracing all parts of your self. Here, you can see and taste life fully, participating consciously with it all, becoming a co-creator of yourself and of the entire universe.

The opening and healing of the womb is a unique and personal experience, with common threads experienced by each person as they go on this journey deep into their original self, the collective of humanity, and beyond. Below are some of the comments from people all over the world as they stepped through the doorway into their womb.

Infinite gratitude for doing the work and returning sacred practices of the Divine Feminine, which I have always felt existed and which I once practiced, to me. (A. S.)

Thank you for receiving us . . . women. You reflect the Divine Masculine in holding the space for us to emerge in Grace. Thank you so much. What you do you can't put a price on, and I am truly grateful. (D. J.)

It was very intense, very spiritual, very physical, very emotional, and very full of integrity. I personally faced many things that were lingering . . . many strengths that were evolving and many unexplained things that needed to be faced in order to evolve further. (J. S.)

Although I'm open, I can be a bit of a skeptic, and to experience firsthand the power of these simple ancient practices was mind-blowing. I was able to feel so clearly our underlying unity—and the power that is within all of us individually to heal ourselves and the world, in a very real way. For myself, I feel now the beauty, the importance, and the real possibility of coming into my own power. It's brought me to re-envision my view of power and my way of being in the world, to open myself up to the power of the feminine. Yes! In all its soft, loving, deep, dark, fiery, creative entirety. And to see, more largely, the importance of bringing that energy into the world now. (W. C.)

It was painful, but when the pain was gone it was heaven! Bliss and joy, tears and laughter . . . what I received was love! It seems that what I had to learn about myself is whatever happens in my life unconditional love is the way to go. (E. V. D. B.)

Infinite gratitude for bringing back and facilitating the Divine Feminine . . . I feel the boundless nature of my womb, and that my power, the Power of the Womb and of Woman, has now returned to me. My whole system is shaking, as though with labor pains if giving birth to a child—I felt the same as when I gave birth to my two sons. Thanks for all your sacred safe support and guiding! It was a deep cleaning up . . . by liquid light. (U. W.)

I could feel physically the healing in my womb, the energy changing, I felt it on my first and second chakras, on the front and back . . . my body temperature dropped . . . I was freezing. I felt changes on my throat, and the whole body suspended in time and space. Both Monday and today there is a deep sadness that seems not to stop. (R. P.)

The three days were life-changing. I met with a wonderful, supportive group of people that helped me step in to my own power and move to the next level. (N. S.)

I have stepped in to my true power as a co-creator and manifester; the Divine Feminine is powerfully present and flowing through me now in a tangible way. It was the final preparation I needed to be complete within myself and finally be able to meet my divine partner. All the things I have wanted to create or have dreamed of having in my life are finally falling into place around me as I sit in wonder and amazement and graceful receptivity. This got me in touch with my true power, creativity, and dharma/purpose for this incarnation that I have long felt drawing near but was only now totally aware of. (A. T.)

I used to have this fear that as soon as I would truly ground myself, I would lose my light. Now I know that I can never lose the light, for the light is a part of me (as is the shadow). I can now inhabit earth and experience all (light and dark) without the fear of losing myself. Another thing I gained is the trust that I can express myself and the Divine through myself anytime I want to or feel like it. It is no longer hard; on the contrary, it is pure joy! (S. V.)

What was once unplugged, disconnected, forgotten, has now returned to wholeness. In reflections on myself before awakening to Shakti, I sense suffering, isolation, numbness, separation. I tune in now and am amazed at the dance that has taken place within my soul; one that now will never cease to be danced. To feel the flow of light moving on its own, breathing on its own throughout my being is a precious gift to behold. In just sitting quietly now, everything feels different. The 18 points of the pathway feel electric when I tune in to them, whereas before they were just simply parts of the body. The flow among them all is regenerating a charged current through my field and this makes the body feel viscerally different, more alive even in stillness. (T. A.)

When I tune in from the yoni to the deep inner spaces of the womb, I realize what a deep healing has taken place. There is a pregnant emptiness there, as if it is ready to create because the slate is now clean. There is also a deep peace, not just within the gates, but within all the cells of the body, an invigorated peace, a vibrant stillness unlike any I have known or reached in years of meditation. The earth herself feels different somehow as well, as though her gates have been healed, cleared, and activated too.

Through the exercises and focused intent, I feel the praise, gratitude, and compassion that I should feel as part of the Divine Woman. It feels as if the entire meaning of being a woman has been brought back to its original intent. (C. O.)

There has always been a hesitancy, a holding back, keeping the fires controlled, living in the comfort zone of nurturing, supporting, giving to, and loving others, unaware of the selfishness that dwelled within that zone, that served the need to be loved, needed, and validated. Honoring the Light of our Being and skirting or turning away from the Darkness is what we were taught. Until now, there have been no teachings shared to take us into the vast realms of the Black Light [the purest and richest form of Divine Love]. There had been no understanding of the power of the womb, a power that remained hidden behind the iron doors created from within and through patriarchy into the collective consciousness of humanity. (K. M.)

There is a softness that has imbued my being more fully and more profoundly than I have ever experienced. Women, out of our historical and genetic patterns, and related to all of our past incarnations, tend to emerge based either on the side of power or on the side of love. Whichever the case, to move into our truth and balance, it is the opposite quality that we have to find within ourselves again. Moving into the Compassionate Womb and the Light River, I have found a wellspring of peace deep within that allows me to soften and to perceive in a totally different way. It is a peace that is imbued with empathy and acceptance, a beautiful softness that makes me feel truly feminine as I never have before; and grateful in a new way for everything in and around me. It has stirred within me an understanding of the deeper levels of compassion and love that we are capable of as true reflections of God in human form. (T. A.)

The right workshop, the right person, the right time. The way you dealt with the whole matter was very profound. Now my womb feels empty and clean, and my whole body is vibrating. (W. M.)

> *Padma Prakasha is a rare find. He has the unique ability to transport your body, mind, and soul to the next octave of consciousness with his words of wisdom, heartfelt questions, and vast love for everyone he meets. Padma's ability to tap into the heart of the ancient mysteries and to articulate their modern-day message to us humans is amazing. Reading this material or attending his seminars and retreats will rock your world, and monumental change is always imminent once being in his presence.*
>
> LINDA STAR WOLF, AUTHOR OF *SHAMANIC BREATHWORK* AND DIRECTOR OF VENUS RISING INSTITUTE FOR SHAMANIC HEALING ARTS

As you can see, it is a palpably visceral experience to step through the womb. It takes courage to face the unknown and keep going.

5
Restoring the Sacredness of the Womb

Listening to the Voice Within

The womb is a sanctified, precious space. In ancient times it was known as the holy of holies, the inner sanctum where only one man was allowed to venture, and to enter, to create the vibration that would fertilize and germinate the vast, infinite, formless potential that lies dormant within each and every woman. The womb is the heart of the feminine temple, the heart of the feminine vision, the heart of the feminine prophecy and oracle guiding the way from darkness into light and from light into darkness.

It is the womb that is the woman's Guru. It is the womb that is your original voice, not relying on a transcendent god outside of you, but the direct voice of God within you, separate from the mind, indeed a foreigner to the mind, a whole, unique voice, a distinct chord playing in the music that creates a woman's body, soul, and mind. It is this chord that holds together a woman's body, mind, and spirit; it is the interface, the connector, between each separate part of a woman.

When all parts of you connect through the womb, then all parts of you can dance and play together. The womb is the conductor of your orchestra; if all energies coming into you go through the womb, then that will connect everything else. If there is some energy not being assimilated or accepted by the womb, then that part of you will also not be connected within you.

The womb is a gateway, a portal, for everything to enter you, and for everything to leave you. Everything plugs into the womb, and from the womb connects to everything else. So be careful what you plug into, and what you allow in. Be careful that what you plug into, and allow in, is right for you, for it fully becomes part of you.

Without being fully plugged into the womb there are parts of you that are fragmented, alone, shattered, disconnected, and separate. Joining and uniting all the parts of your heart-womb through this focus, this lens, requires a conscious effort on your behalf for the body to flush out, energize, clear, and heal. Be mindful of the womb as you rise, and as you go to sleep. Check on it, and make sure it is clear and happy. Run the events and occurrences, interactions, and feelings of the day through the womb, and see what she says. She allows you to respond to life in a clear, joyful, life-enhancing manner.

NAMING THE WOMB

After clearing and connecting to the womb, you are ready to receive the name of your womb. Knowing the name of our womb allows you to initiate clear communication with your womb, which has its own innate wisdom and guidance independent of the mind and your conditioning.

It is your primal voice, and a lot different in most cases to the guidance you normally receive through the mind. It is your original voice, untainted and empowered, knowing what nurtures it and what harms it. It can guide you to your further empower-ment if you speak with her and act on her guidance. The more you act on her guidance, the stronger she will become; the more you speak with her, the more she will empower you into your true feminine nature, into your full womanhood.

Your womb is normally the size of a pear. Place your hands in an inverted triangle position over the womb, just under your belly button.

Focus your attention to the area created by your hands, and breathe deeply into your belly. Focus the energy of each breath into this place, and with each breath deepen the focus to go deeper inside.

Now ask your womb what her name is and listen for the reply. It may come instantly; it may not. Simply be receptive and ask. It may not have a name you have ever heard before, as most wombs have names in sacred languages, like Sanskrit, Hebrew, or Egyptian. Simply be open, and ask.

When you have received the name of your womb, start to speak to her as you would a dear friend. Ask her questions. As your dialogue deepens, you may receive unusual answers that you have not heard of or thought of before. Go with it, and experiment. Get to know this important part of yourself. The more you do, the more she will share with you.

You can speak to your womb at any time of the day or night. Just place your hands on her, and ask. Soon you will not even have to do this, as your rapport will be instant. For example, if your womb's name is Uma, simply ask Uma what she feels about your latest partner, project, career move, child, or the next healing or step in your life that will take you forward. You can also ask about mundane everyday things, like the right drink or thing to eat, the correct turning in the road, the right way to ask someone something—she is open to anything and everything, from the most banal to the most mystical. Ask and you shall receive.

Passionate Willingness

The love that carries us through the second spiral manifests through willingness. In willingness, one begins to truly care, and wish to give to others. The heart emerges in feelings of love, compassion, and the desire to do things well, for the positive effects upon others and the world. This is a spontaneous feeling arising within you, a welling up and giving guided by a mysterious inner impulse, extending itself gracefully without anyone having to convince you, and no sense of "should."

You become easily and enthusiastically inspired to start making bigger changes. Good results start to come from your endeavors, and this fuels you to keep going, to continue being open and willing, to continue your practice and discipline. Talent, even genius, may be there, but it is only through discipline that you will make anything of it. In this willingness, you say *yes* to life, growth, creativity, and service. You begin to discover the joy of change, of growth. You follow your heart's desire; you have tasted the divine and want more. You become a dedicated, passionate human making sure things get done, and not just talked about.

> *Upon opening into the second spiral of my womb, I began to experience the rampaging onslaught of the true meaning of duality. It was a kind of madness, and its pitch was feverish. My oh so beautiful loving lifestyle had descended into hell. My shadow was fully present, being seen and spoken, and it wasn't pretty. Yet, by trusting the process, I knew it was essential that I continue to work thoroughly and deeply into these unseen aspects. I was well versed and fully equipped with these teachings on how move forward, safely and swiftly.*
>
> *As time passed, a more grounded sense of my womanhood took root; a more mature form of enduring love was being birthed. A stronghold was establishing itself deep within my womb and heart, a place to come from, a place to stand firm in, when all of life seems to be against you. I was needing nothing, other than to love. A trust so vast and true was flowing through me. I was becoming . . . .*
>
> *My Beloved is a powerful man, created with honor, loyalty, and knowingness, yet we entered a moment on our journey when he too, had to step back and allow the fullness of what I was becoming to take her rightful place. (A. A.)*

Evolution always takes the next step forward. On a personal scale, this is your next transformation, your next breakthrough. On a collective level this occurs when a new human being is created and manifested, which is when a new world will be born. On a cosmic level this is when new creations, stars and galaxies are born that have never been birthed before.

Passion is the force behind this evolutionary shift, for passion is love put into action. Passion is life, identifying with the essential basic spark, the will to live which is the will to share, to create; the beginning of life itself. This passion is when we seize life, when we want to be here, and to be who we truly are.

This passion is a will to being; a will to share being. It is the love that seeks the well-being and the full being of all. It is the action that springs from the deep core of our heart, from where our hidden goodness arises and shows itself in our actions, sharing its joy with others in this dynamic manner. This passion is an urgency to continue evolution, to grow it further so we can be more of who we truly are. The universe is expanding as are we, constantly, in every moment. To align to this wave means we continually and perpetually redefine who we are in order to embrace and expand to the highest potential available in any moment.

Passion comes from love. It is the passion, and love for the best in yourself and others that leads you into divine will, the will that is larger than your own, and which leads you to your highest potential. Love and passion becomes a force that when combined with humility and creativity becomes a force for total revolution. Evolution becomes the revolution.

It is purpose, passion, and love that fuels you, which burns inexhaustibly within you, and pulls you through any and all things. Once you taste this possibility, faith deepens, and this in turn fuels it further. This passion can never be taken away; it is always there. This passion is the conviction that deeply feels for all beings, welling up from deep in the core of the heart to help all beings move forward. The passion for total revolution is not for the timid, those who keep themselves small, and those who are not completely honest.

Passion arises in those who truly love truth and will do whatever it takes to live, breathe, and share that more. For when we abandon ourselves to being an evolutionary agent, unlimited energy flows through us. This passion cannot be faked. It is the instant openness and willingness to embrace the highest potential in any moment and to move that moment forward with others as a part of that embracing. It is the catalyst that sparks and ignites the slumbering of others marooned in their comfort zones, happy to keep to their illusion of a personal enlightenment.

> *For some of us there comes a moment when you cry out: I want God more than anything else, I want truth, I want love, and I am willing to face anything to realize that! This is a true moment.*
>
> *This is what I call "an essential experience," a moment in which there is a shift in consciousness. And it is essential because until that moment, all talk of being "true" or "vigilant" or "telling the truth" is abstract, like something you would learn in class. None of this can have concrete meaning in your life until you have had this experience. With this shift in consciousness, what was not known is suddenly seen. And this recognition is the luck of a lifetime. It is a blessing of a lifetime. It is grace coming out.*
>
> *That recognition is the beginning. This is a radical business but a joyful business, a simple business. But it is not for the fainthearted. It takes the courage of a lifetime, because everything in us, all of our conditioning says "No, no. Don't go there. Don't touch that. Don't do that." And yet when you reach a certain stage of yearning, everything in your lifetime is saying "I have to, I have to discover the truth, have to know, have to be true." And then you will see where your allegiance is, where your attention is. (A. A.)*

It is the initiative to dare, to break boundaries, to ignore social mores and etiquette, to break new ground, and to break people into this new ground in the most direct way possible. It is the power of clarity that opens the pathway for evolution to occur, allied with the willingness for all to be equal and to share their piece at any moment.

Deep passion in its evolutionary expression is the urge to want to bring people together, for the basic pattern of evolution is to unite in order to create. Passion for evolution, for God, is what brings creative unions together. It is through passion that egos dissolve in creative free flow, connecting the dots that unite disparate pieces of the global puzzle to form a cohesive unity where souls unite without egoistic agendas, beliefs, and feelings of lack, threat, or inadequacy, dissolving boundaries to reveal and create the next step in evolution.

When people are masters within themselves, and/or of a particular field of expertise, they have inner knowing and sublime confidence. Then they can delight in meeting and creating with other masters to create something far greater than any of them alone could possibly ever imagine, or achieve. Here a master can take notes and make the tea if another is flowing with Spirit's creative outpouring at that moment, as they are all egoless and committed to the one that is flowing in the living field of energy created when "two or more are gathered in my name." Yet the level of light that any single group can bring into the world is limited only by the vision, and thoughts, held in the mind of each of its members.

Consciousness is evolving, and in that evolution is creating the foundations for an enlightened civilization. The whole of evolution now rests squarely on our shoulders, for we are evolution. To do this requires a real thinking out of the box approach, birthed out of the new moment or out of the blue; something simple but radical that has never been done before. Something that links the common threads we all share, regardless of caste, creed, religion and cultural preferences, and elevates this to a whole new octave. Here we have to experiment with the impossible in order to make it possible, by manifesting it through our own choice, our volunteering to work together as one.

In our zest for life, we bring the future into the present. This attraction, this passion, this love, is what makes evolution possible as a sustained reality rather than just glimpses of what is, or what could be. This is the promise of this age and the pinnacle of evolution; to make time serve us, to use time wisely to extend and share the good, the holy and the truthful, for time has been created for the purposes of evolution, to serve the evolutionary impulse.

Today this can only happen through a collective union that is drawn together by a single all-attracting influence that we all share in, that can bring us all together. The return of the womb is a big part of this, as without the womb nothing new can birth.

THE PLACENTA: OUR FIRST CORD OF CONNECTION*

When we are in the womb as a fetus we are surrounded by the placenta, which nourishes and sustains us until we are ready to step out and be born into this world. Placenta and baby both arise from the very same cell, the fertilized ovum, and in one sense that makes baby and placenta one, sharing the same etheric field.

The placenta is the first mother to each of us. It feeds us and is there for us, providing all we need to grow. Placenta is our sustainer and protector, our first love felt in the body, the first experience of unconditional love we receive. When we are cut off from this first source of love prematurely, it leads to us seeking love outside of our own self, in a conditional way.

Sadly, this is what happens to more than 99 percent of us when our umbilical cord is prematurely cut when we are born, because we are separated from our life force and soul connection, which is still pulsing through the cord connecting us to the placenta. This cut happens before the placenta has transferred its emotional nurturing qualities and soul essence to us. This sudden separation creates shock and fear, borne out of ignorance for the deeper connection between life, love, mother, and child.

The loss, abandonment, and grief that we can experience in our unformed bodies and minds as we enter this world brutally and prematurely cut off from the nurturing, unconditionally loving envelope of the placenta is a huge conditioning for us. We actually experience separation for the first time in the bodymind in this action of cutting the umbilical cords, for before this, placenta, womb, baby, and mother were one. It is our first separation in this world.

As adults you can heal this separation within yourself through a placenta healing, which hundreds of men and women who have experienced this healing can testify to. Indeed, this chapter is based on these men and women's experiences of the placenta healing method, which reconnects

*This is similarly discussed in my book *The Power of Shakti,* pages 159–66.

the umbilical cord back to Source. This healing was originally used by the priestesses of Isis in Egypt, and it has been given again to humanity by this lineage in order to accelerate reconnection to the Source within.

The feeling of deep peace, softness, nurturance, being comforted, and held gently yet powerfully in this wound reintroduces this frequency back to our bodymind and soul, uniting them. The effects of this can be both "wonderful and frightening," as D. K. reports. For him, it "felt at first as if I was in the womb, surrounded by peace and love . . . a time before any thought. Then I experienced being born. The umbilical cord was cut and I experienced much fear and terror. I felt separate. I had a hard time catching my breath. Finally, I was able to breathe through the fear and terror. Then again I felt the peace and love surrounding me, except this time it came from within, and not from without."

The body, mind, and soul can really feel how big this trauma is, for when we feel cut off from the umbilical cord, we feel cut off from the information of love. "I feel my placenta is my own connection to the love of the universe and a divine connection to other human beings. It's my first connection to universal, unconditional love." When the cord is cut too early, one woman experienced "a deep loneliness, sadness, emptiness, and loss."

When you are cut off from the feeling of love so early in life, many beliefs arise to fill this hole. For some people who have experienced the healing of their placenta, such beliefs can include the feeling of "I could be abandoned every time I'm in a relationship so I feel I have put on many subterfuges to not be abandoned."

The inner battle between liking and disliking one's self, self-love and self-hatred, also arises. As one woman put it, "The following day I literally fell in love with myself! It was a very new feeling to me. . . . I don't how to explain but I felt there wasn't anymore a separation between me and myself. I used to feel a little disconnected with who I am, maybe not really accepting who I am. I felt I was back into myself. I wasn't harsh to myself anymore . . . I was kind to myself."

The feelings of softness, warmth, kindness, and gentleness return to this part of yourself that has been forgotten, and most importantly, unnurtured. The healing of this separation can re-evoke in us the cellular memory of being connected, of being nurtured by the mother, that gives us security in life, in our own loving and nurturing capacities, and in intimate relationship.

As M. C. puts it, "The energy that pulses through the cord from the placenta is the Divine Mother nourishing us. It is neither wholly our biological mother's nor ours alone, but something that connects us to one another and to the Divine Mother. This divine energy is transferred to us, into our bodies by the mother through the placenta. Regardless of how our biological mothers feel or who they are, the divine wants us to thrive more than anything.

"The energy we receive while in the womb is what brings Spirit into us. It is the part that can save us from destroying everything . . . it is possibly as close as we can get to Spirit before our souls are fully awakened. It is, in effect, a great mystery and miracle. The Divine Mother is in and around all of us—we all have the most wonderful mother, as loving as we can imagine and beyond."

Letting the placenta drop off and release by itself, usually between three to seven days after being born, leads to peace and the wisdom "I receive," "I have everything I need," "Everything is here and now." As another woman put it, "I'm connected to unconditional love of the Source and nothing, never could cut that. I feel myself in security: I'm loved!"

Gaia's Cord

In Cambodia the placenta is known as "the globe of the origin of the soul," and for the Maori it is *te whenua* (the land) that nourishes the people, as does the *whenua* (placenta) of the woman. Mother, child, and land are all intimately interconnected, each nourishing and sustaining the other. When one is looked after, the others benefit also. All are interconnected from the moment of conception itself! This living connection establishes and sustains the vital personal and soul link between the land and the child, and among the human soul, physical body, and life force.

When this connection is not honored, mother, child, and land all suffer, as life itself is not being respected, nurtured, and cared for. In consciously keeping the connection between placenta and child by not cutting the cord and by burying the placenta underground (and by having the mother connect to the land as well through ceremony), the living threads of energy that interconnect and sustain ourselves, our community, and Gaia weave us together in the web of life and love.

In healing the umbilicus trauma, we can reconnect with this cord of love that roots us into Gaia, triggering the remembrance in our body's cellular memory. As Sue shares, "My body was heavy . . . going into the earth. As I sat with this energy I was visited by three indigenous souls. The longer I sat quietly, the deeper the stillness, the deeper the peace, and the more connected into body and earth I became . . . very nurturing and blessed."

Twin Souls

In many sacred traditions the placenta is seen as our twin soul, our double. The Baganda of Uganda believe that the placenta is actually a second child, the child's double, with the placenta also having its own soul that resides in the umbilical cord. Ancient Egyptian pharaohs believed one soul inhabited the body, the other the placenta, with the placenta respected and honored as their guardian, and as their twin from birth; a valued part of themselves, not separate or useless.*

The umbilicus connection holds this aspect of our twin soul or divine double connection, because the first experience we have on the earth plane of our twin soul is the placenta. When the trauma of this separation is healed we can deeply relax and let go as we find this connection within ourselves and no longer feel so drawn to finding it outside. We feel our own source of nourishment and deep inner peace,

*In the Old Testament the placenta was thought to be the External Soul.

comfort, and contentment that we may look outside for in intimate relationship, within us.

HEALING OUR FIRST CORD OF CONNECTION

Deep emotion and tears are common during and after the umbilicus healing, as are physical discharges from the womb, fatigue, headaches, womb cramping, and physical pains and stiffness. This is because the severing of the cord creates a false body attitude in all of us. When the energetic cause of this false attitude is removed, the body can return to more of its natural, healed state. These symptoms arise because of this split between body and mind and are healed by the reintroduction of the soft, enveloping feeling of the placenta's nurturing energy being remembered on the physical level, which creates shifts in conjunction with the body's innate wisdom. As H. T. put it, "I feel I'm making peace with my physical body."

After a placenta healing, many people feel a great sense of wellness encoded in their bodies. Expanded states of peace also arise with the feeling that something has finally come to rest deep within them: the cord that was cut has now been reconnected to its source. As J. H. put it, "It was as if my whole inner being, my self, was gone, joining the deepest part one can search for and being welcome there. This very soft and wonderful vibration traveled all over my body . . . there were no boundaries, just intense light."

As L. P. put it, "The energy I experienced was very soft, flowing very sweet, gentle but powerful, and cleared out a lot of *samskaras* [imprintings]." As C. O. recounted, "It felt as my womb felt after giving birth, as an emptying without the intense contractions, a warmth of the flow of something, similar to the bleeding in menses. In my emotional body there was the sense of letting go of something that has been with me my entire physical life."

Remembering this essence on a cellular level is, according to D. W., like "a deep basking in the inner light: very sweet. I am becoming significantly less engaged with external drama . . . getting triggered by the world around me far less. I am experiencing lovely feelings of contentment and a sense of being supported by my own Source, the inner light feels near and accessible. I also seem to have had a breakthrough in terms of my tendencies to judge those around me." In this reclaiming we can experience that "recurrent feelings of shame, self-judgment and self-worthlessness are simply gone: I do not react to triggers with an automatic response anymore," as U. C. stated.

The placenta healing can aid the psychosomatic healing of family and ancestral issues that tend to linger on into our adult lives. For U. C., who had done a lot of healing on her mother's issues but was unable to break through her inherited family dysfunctions, "healing the placenta also means healing the information that was passed from mother to child in utero. The relief I now feel from this healing is indescribable. I feel that I can now move on and get out in the world in action . . . so that feels like being born, quite simply."

In many births the balance between the energetic and physical is disrupted by the physical placenta being removed, yet still the remaining cords to the energetic placenta continue to hold connection to the child's soul. In order to complete this unfinished part of the process we have to heal the energetic placenta, reconnect the cord, and let go. To bring resolution to the process of the spirit-placenta reconnection means that both the child's soul and the mother's soul are laid to rest, healing, restoring, and regenerating Shakti.

You can remedy the placenta disconnection through gentle, loving, natural birth practices for your own children. When allowance is given for the umbilical cord to drop away naturally after birth, all the life force of the placenta gets transferred along the cord to the baby, and the etheric field around baby and placenta is sealed off properly. This complete field results in a stronger immune system and the baby feeling safe, nurtured, respected, and balanced. Baby feels supported and nurtured and ready to make the step into this world in a safe, secure, loving way that suits the child's rhythms. By doing this, you can help your children to not be run by programs and fears of scarcity, loss, and insecurity that we too have experienced. The scientific studies done on children who have not had their umbilical cord cut prematurely show that these infants are more peaceful, less disruptive, and better behaved.

PART THREE

The Third Spiral

6
The Womb of All Attraction

The Pathway through the Shadow Self

The women living in the third spiral live in joy with much energy, vitality, and a glowing womb. Sacred sensuality is embodied, and the sexual energy channels in the body-mind-soul system are open and flowing. Shakti and light force flows through the body and womb as creative power increases with clarity. The magnetic intensity of the womb activates and manifests, attracting all that it needs. The womb can literally manifest whatever it desires when it is aligned with the heart and your divine blueprint.

The breath penetrates deep down, and a great gateway is reached. The bridge is found, and now one needs to step across it. Every journey of soul consequence begins at a doorway, face to face with a guardian or a test. Once we make the commitment to pass through the doorway, to go through the fire, to have the bravery to step in to the unknown, even though it may be frightening, we start to encounter a deeper, intuitive knowing about something else. This bridge into a vaster reality is what the third spiral opens you into.

When one encounters this power, one can run away, embrace the lesson and/or find joy and great laughter. Any dishonesty and masking of the self, any place where you do not love and accept yourself, any place where you are unaware of a need for change, will arise. This can be a tough journey but does eventually lead to joy and a powerfully loving, content state of resolution and centering.

The third spiral was the battleground of all my relationships with earthly matters. It was here that I confronted my full-on resistance to continue onward, and it was here that the entire spectrum of my emotions became ravishingly potent.

Love and devotion became nearly overwhelming to the point of passing out, and the flip side of that coin was that anger and frustration were at an all-time high too! What I came to realize is this: as we do Womb Work and face the shadow, bringing ourselves back into reunion with our true feminine center, emotion becomes purified. Now this doesn't mean at first that all the negative feelings dissolve into love and happiness, oh no! As we begin to love more, so too do we find the sobriety to die to our old ways.

Anger becomes purified, not seething with hatred, revenge, or justification as it was before we came to this work. All the buildup is stripped bare by this stage, and now we are left with clean and fresh anger. This experience is fast and wild, yet within moments it is done and dusted. Cleanly seen, felt, and then released.

When you do this for the first couple of times you can actually splutter, choke, gag, or cough as you leverage the deep, dense emotion up and out of the physical body and safely deliver it to the heart. The heart knows exactly what to do with this. No burden is too large, or too gross. The heart does what it does best, love and embrace.

This does not mean that these demons from the dungeon become accepted and held within the safety of the heart, where no questions are asked. It simply means that the power of love penetrates and transforms the bitterness and destruction with its all-consuming potent light. It is not to wipe out our suffering, but to find a channel for it. (A. A.)

THE MEETING OF LIGHT AND DARK

In the third spiral one finds the pathway through the shadow self, which one can only walk through by total dedication to Self with the ability to give all you have in your search, without hesitation, without holding back. One has to give all to receive all. The third spiral is where light and dark meet. It is the bridge and can lead you to both positive and negative outcomes as it is the gateway to the rich mine of spiritual wealth known as the Golden Shadow—where our highest potential lies.

The third spiral not only soothes us but also provokes our egos, breaking our boundaries and limiting belief systems that subtly control our lives in order to liberate us into our highest potential. The demands of this upon you can be unorthodox, as it is not only a guiding energy but also a transforming one. It matures you through unifying opposing forces within you.

> *I see the third spiral as a little death. The little self has to die to who it was, who it wished to be, along with all its achievements and successes, claims to fame and falsities—false beauty, false love, false illumination, false peace, and false joy. Recognize any of them? It is in the third spiral that we see these false prophets and can, like I did, drop to your knees with despair. Ah the cover has been blown! Isn't it beautiful how all this works? (A. A.)*

The third spiral has no qualms or ideas of good and bad as it sees them both as coming from the same source: the power of our highest human potential. The third spiral is the portal to the One, accessed when one is at the threshold, the gates of a big breakthrough. It teaches us not to be seeking a cure for our suffering but rather to seek a use for it, a channel to direct this force into, to create something out of it.

The third spiral truly does bring about a great breakthrough. All of your entirety becomes non-judged by yourself. Others may judge you, but that is *their* business and none of yours. Within the third spiral all emotion is seen as simply E-Motion, energy in motion. From the highest forms of love, which we may have held back or managed, to the cruelest and unfair dismissing emotions, all are welcome. Nothing is judged, repressed, or overindulged. If the emotion is destructive, it is dealt with effectively with grace and acknowledgment.

> *It was during the transition through the third spiral that one of my greatest breakthroughs happened! I have always been a being with a well-rounded sexual repertoire. It was this arena that provided the backdrop for me to learn who I was sexually as I moved through my twenties and thirties. It was also providing a backdrop yet again as I ventured into this journey known as Womb Wisdom.*
>
> *So, in the present day, here I was fully living in the heart, with a loving appetite for sexual pleasures and divine lovemaking, when I begin to hear the familiar knock at the door of my old sexual self. Unresolved ghosts that needed expression, without judgment or taboo, that makes things naughty and somehow desirable to the shadow.*
>
> *My old self wasn't too bothered whether it was love making, or good old-fashioned sex! Both the sexual urge and desire of the lower self, and the heart's wishes to unite in divine love with God as the third, have to come together. They can only come together with the free play and acceptance of all sides, sex and soul. It is here that we experience and encounter the merging of the white and dark rivers of our sexual soul, found in every woman.*
>
> *In the third spiral, the fullness of love opens to include all forms of all sexual behavior and play. I was quite taken back with the width of this embrace. It was such a huge relief to allow my darkest desires to be accepted and played out in love. It truly was a RIP moment. The dark river needs to feel love in order to unite with the light river, and the white river embraces, accepts, and holds dear the desires of the dark river. Both opposing forces unite in order to open the womb further. Nothing can be left out. (A. A.)*

THE OPEN WOMB

The third spiral is known as the Womb of All Attraction, as it is where intense magnetism and sensual attraction occur. When the womb is open in the third spiral, the energies that emanate from her can be alluring, tempting, and seductive to man and woman. It can drive people crazy, wild with desire, wild with jealousy, wild with anger; it can also bring man and woman to their knees in prostration, in reverence, in service.

It intensifies and exaggerates all polarities, which is why many womb rituals are done in secret. Women had to protect themselves from being abused and manipulated. However, others can go into admiration, reverence and service, recognizing the living holiness and preciousness of the person.

What occurred previously in history is that women reached this stage with men servicing and loving them, and then they chose, as groups of women, to go and abuse that power for purposes of control and domination. In this it became unbalanced; it became power hungry, megalomaniacal; it become a quest for power instead of union between beloveds working in harmony, hand in hand with each other in order to create in alignment with the divine blueprint, rather than their own will.

It is this level that many women have memories of, and it is also where they got stuck. Many wombs incarnate today have reached this point and then fallen astray, unable to make the next step into full compassion and union for the benefit of all beings; unable to go to the next step where they are able to manifest the whole.

Age-old cycles of matriarchy and patriarchy have continued to repeat on earth due to the unbalanced nature of the male-female dynamic, which leads to the abuse of power. The manipulation and abuse of men by women, through woman's more subtle seductions, and women by men by the more overt, violent, and direct route, have repeated in a vicious loop for millennia.

The release of thoughtforms and memories within the womb on both a personal and collective level add to this field as the floodgates open and the woman becomes more and more sensitive and open to the web of life.

THE SEVEN GATES TO THE GRAIL WOMB*

The seven gateways hold a powerful, timeless pathway to feminine truth, a pathway that has been forgotten and is now being remembered again, for the seven gates are a key to embodying the Grail within. The seven gates were originally known and practiced by the priestesses of Isis and were used to empower and guide women into experiencing and using their full life force through the crucible of the womb. This then enabled them to empower men into the divine masculine, to initiate men into many aspects of life, from lovemaking, sacred union, and birthing to co-creation and the balance between male and female. To initiate a man into this spaciousness and presence required that he enter a fully open womb through these seven gates.

The womb is the crucible of creation. Each woman holds this loving power to create and manifest from her own womb, which becomes the portal to the Cosmic Womb from which all creation springs and into which all dissolves back. Knowledge of the womb is one of the last great mysteries to be revealed in this age, although it has been known and used in the past in cultures such as the Mayan, Tibetan, Indian, Gnostic Christian, and Egyptian, among others.

The seven gates are a set of energetic portals that open the way into the womb. They form a channel from the yoni to the G-spot, or gratitude spot, to the clitoris, moving through the cervix into the womb and the fifth, sixth, and seventh gates—the spaciousness of the Cosmic Womb. When healed, nourished, remembered, and honored as sacred, these seven gates become a royal road into the Grail of the womb: they

*This is similarly discussed in my book *The Power of Shakti,* pages 56–58.

become the keys to manifestation of the Divine Feminine, the keys to Creation itself.

Each gate opens as you progressively heal each part of the yoni and womb, making them sacred portals once again. As each gate opens, one by one, the level of openness and ability to experience love, overflowing embrace and surrender also deepens. This deepening occurs in direct relationship to what you are able to let *in,* to the extent that you are able to be physically, emotionally, and spiritually vulnerable.

The palpable presence of these gates has been forgotten, lost within. The power of woman that you hold deep within her body is right here; all you need is a gentle reminder, a loving touch, to begin the process of making sacred what you already have innately within you. With gentle focus on each gate, touching it with your breath, feel the sparking of the life force at each threshold. Love and bathe each gate with conscious presence, igniting and firing its reawakening and true purpose.

Touching the Lips of Love—the first gate at the threshold of the yoni—massaging them into fullness, opens the pathway to the second gate. This gate, known as the G-spot, or gratitude spot, is wreathed in streaming waterfalls, cascading through every cell of your body. Bathed in love, its sensuality amplifies and readies you for the third gate, the blooming red rose of the clitoris, velvet to the touch, the pleasure of true love and the deep sensitivity to loving and being loved.

This rose leads you to surrender to the river flowing to the fourth gate, the cervix, the portal to the womb, a star gate, a sacred diamond opening. Crossing through this portal into the vastness of womb, you can feel the peace and remember. In that knowing, journey through gates five, six, and seven, through the great central sun to the source of being: the Grail within. It is a memory within every cell of your being.

The seven gates stir memories of the power that manifests within. Integration of these memories is a key to opening and crossing each threshold. Allowing yourself to be penetrated by a male consciousness is the key to opening *all* of the gates *if* you are in a physical relationship. However, many female mystics have opened some of the gates through surrendering to God in a personal form, such as a lover of Krishna (a *gopi*) would, or like female Christian mystics who asked for, and were penetrated by, the Holy Spirit. However, in today's world of interconnection and the embodiment that only an intimate physical relationship can provide, the main way to access this is through committed relating between man and woman.

Such a journey can lead to an experience both of greatest love and profoundest healing.

The Polyp: A Physical Manifestation of the Seven Gates Healing

The first time I embarked on a conscious relationship, all that I have ever known, and all that I had ever learned, had to go. Nothing could ever be referred to, contrasted against, and for sure, never compared with. Sacred Union is only ever once in a lifetime. It is impossible to enter when you are carrying your past, and an idea of who you think you are. The two people have to enter in their entirety, in a sweet innocence yet a fiery passion that will consume them both as they merge and create the alchemy of Divine Marriage.

When my beloved entered me for the first time, my entire being paid immediate attention. My yoni, womb, heart, and brain knew in their fullness that light merged with love had entered my system. A new pathway was being carved out, pushing aside the old tried-and-tested ways of making love, or as I discovered, having sex dressed up as making love.

I remember a deep pain being felt—physical, emotional, and soulful. Something was being "touched" that had never known another or been touched before. This touch created life and vitality in a once dormant cave. I had never truly felt before in my yoni and womb until this moment.

My uterus ached, and lovemaking was uncomfortable. I breathed deeply to allow my internal structure to open and trust this new love in my partner and in myself to be freed. After making love, there was a loss of blood from inside my cervix. This wasn't because we were being boisterous or physically passionate. It was because as I was trusting and breathing, I was opening and allowing him into an access usually denied. For two months I would bleed after lovemaking, and my moon cycles had completely fallen out of rhythm. I was having cycles every two weeks.

It was during this time that I began my shadow work, as I ventured through the seven gates. Mysterious and dark memories were arising as I descended into my shadowy inner world. Hellish places and macabre beings were waiting for my acknowledgment. Twisted and tormented aspects of myself were recapitulated and taken home, back to my Soul.

The personal shadow broke down and into the collective shadow. All these aspects, all these battlefields were, of course, my deeper psyche. So much healing was taking place as lifetimes of hell and darkness were being welcomed home, into the heart of forgiveness and embrace.

In the outer world, I felt that no one could know what I was experiencing. As I closed my eyes, the shadow appeared. With guidance I learned to approach my shadow and pick her off the floor from a dark, cold, and damp cave. She was totally gray, like a cold, hard statue. Her eyes would glare into mine with a lifeless stare. She had no emotion or warmth whatsoever. There was no soul here, just the accumulation of hatred, hurt, and my own betrayal of myself, my soul, and the sanctity of my womb and sexuality.

Eventually, as we communicated with one another, she agreed to lie in my arms, as I gave her the chance to feel the warmth of my love. I held her as I looked down into her face; her eyes were closed as I watched my teardrops drop onto her cheeks. I could feel "me" inside her; I began to feel our connection. The agony of seeing myself in this form was tearing me apart.

These were the moments when my polyp was being transformed on the inside. I could feel my cellular system amp up a level, the fiber of my being was absorbing so much light as my love began to penetrate and weave its way into the darkest, most lost fragments of my tossed-aside self.

Every time my beloved and I penetrated a deeper physical wall within my yoni, an adjustment would be made, an emotional and spiritual barrier broken, and the bleeding would begin again. Each time one of my seven gates opened, more blood appeared. Each time a new level of love and intimacy arose from within me, more blood appeared, as if washing away the years of self-abuse and animal sexuality that I had engaged in, wishing it were love but not knowing any better.

My health and vitality were normal, and I was not worried about all these physical symptoms, but I was getting concerned that I had started my menopause early.

So I went to the doctor's office to have some health checks. My blood was good, no STDs, hormones perfect, and no early menopause. However, when I had an internal examination something was seen: a polyp, the size of a pea on the end of my cervix. This was the reason for all the bleeding after making love. I was told it had to be removed by a laser!

A polyp is an unexplained surge of creation, where an internal organ decides to begin growth again and create an extra bit on the side. They are harmless, but they have their own blood supply, nerve endings, and tissues. They are just "extra" pieces. So I tuned in to this "extra" piece and meditated on its deeper meaning. I knew instantly that our conscious lovemaking was giving me the opportunity to get rid of all the times I had had sex, gave myself when I didn't want to, took part in sexual acts that I didn't feel comfortable with, and generally gave myself away to those I did not really love or was loved by.

My yoni and womb knew this in their innate intelligence, and many layers of this desensitization I had allowed to occur, all these cellular memories, were accumulated together; and in the body's immaculate intelligence a polyp was formed, to contain all this debris from my past. All those times when I felt lonely, isolated, and not known in sex, those cold and harsh places where sex becomes animalistic, where sex was the only means of communication and a threadbare intimacy, where I had disrespected and abused myself and allowed others to do so with my ignorance.

For weeks, I meditated and gazed into my cervix. I checked in daily and sent waves of forgiveness and presence to my reproductive system. My beloved would bathe me in his love, light, and clarity as we made love, opening the walls and the seven gates with loving power and tender presence. Each time a gate opened we would both feel it as a new level of love arose.

One day I just knew the polyp was gone! My moon cycles had returned to their natural rhythm; all the bleeding had stopped. As only a woman can tell you, I just knew that all was as it should be. When I was examined six weeks later, the doctor, to her amazement, announced the polyp was gone. No need for the laser! I smiled to myself, I just knew it!

The polyp was being used as storage for the debris of my sexual past, as well as my shadow. As I removed all remnants of my old ways of relating, as I became clear, the polyp dissolved and transformed. I believe the polyp had created its own ecosystem. Without relying on the cervix in any way, the polyp worked to recycle and transform the polluted cells, the layers of protection and desensitization that my womb and yoni had created to protect itself from the lack of love and harshness of the men who had been inside me, as well as my own sexual misdemeanors.

When the work was done, the cells returned to my reproductive system and the polyp dissolved, leaving not a trace of its existence anywhere. The past was gone, and my womb was clear enough for the next stage. (A. A.)

The inviting of the masculine essence to come deep into you requires that you become totally vulnerable, opening, embracing, surrendering to, and receiving the male essence in its totality.* How deeply do you trust the masculine? When the seven gates are open, you are letting a man deep into your soul and your feminine essence, fully into the womb consciousness, which also has enormous benefits for him.

This letting in, of course, can only happen through deep mutual intimacy and surrender to the other. When enough sexual, emotional, and heart healing has been done by both partners—both alone and in the mirror of relationship—then this penetration and surrender can occur, organically unfolding the gates. The level of mutual love, trust, commitment, and willingness to grow are key factors in this, as well as the ability of the

*This is similarly discussed in my book *The Power of Shakti,* pages 58–68.

man to be able to support the woman, to be the safe pillar for the woman, therefore letting her go deeper into her own essential feminine nature and deeper into the womb consciousness, taking the masculine with her.

The gates begin with the first gate at the opening of the yoni lips and progress into the seventh gate of the fully open womb. The gates become more like energetic veils of emotion and love when one reaches the fourth gate and beyond, which is the opening into the womb of pure space and infinite potential. At this point, you start to access the subtler energies of the womb and of the *unmanifest*.

One starts to make love in a different way on the subtle planes and goes deeper into bliss. The man becomes swallowed in the infinite womb and surrenders to this drawing inward into the depths where all men wish to go, back to the source of life and original innocence. The man becomes humbled and empowered in a new manner, and the woman rests in ease and deep acknowledgment of her own divine nature, born from the deeper connecting and opening of the womb and heart. Divine Feminine and Divine Masculine are born.

THE TWO RIVERS

A woman can strengthen her individuality when she removes her essential feminine self from the existing social values, family structures, cultural conditionings, and expectations. In separating herself momentarily from the masculine—traditionally done in sacred traditions for a thirteen-day cycle with this intent—she finds her roots in her feminine nature, enabling her to become fully Self contained, empowered, and connected. She finds a foundation in the roots of the Eternal Feminine within her own inner divinity. She accesses a deeper strength, insight, intuition, and her own individual center. This also has deep implications and healing for the man in her life.

This individuality is found and realized by exploring the two rivers flowing through either side of the yoni itself: the dark river and the white river. The free flow of Shakti brings up the dark river, the Black

Goddess of lust, repression, and fear—the bad girl—revealing it, reveling in it, and expressing it until it finds its civilized form, an expression of power and authority centered in Self. Shakti also serves to reveal the ideas of the white river, the ideal of the perfect woman—the good girl—here to do the things expected of her by others. She is pure, holy, a perfect mother, lover, and partner. The true essence of Shakti balances both the dark and light: the two rivers flow through each side of the yoni up into the fourth gate, where the guardians of each river then unite in the opening of the womb.

In this journey we find that the black river can ignite, reveal, transform, and inspire us. In the past this dark river was condemned for its power to enflame women into free expression and embodiment of their sexual power. Many witches were burned for knowing and consciously using this power to create with, and many more women were hung during the Inquisitions for embodying this power.

The white river of purity, holiness, order—the ideal of a civilized woman in her right place—has for many centuries been the accepted cultural norm for what a woman should be. This ideal describes a nice, sweet, loving person without the power to transform herself profoundly, someone incapable of challenging or confronting things beyond the economic or cultural surface, a woman who knows her place in a man's world.

It is fear of the power of the black river that keeps women in the role of the white goddess—running away from full empowerment and full potential. In the times we live in, this form of behavior has run its course, for the black river brings up the deepest darkness, the most powerful wounds you have, and in so doing enables you to reclaim your power fully. The black river fuels both power and love in an embodied, visceral manner.

Shakti brings us what we need in order to grow. Shakti fulfills the desires of those who are pure, by giving rise to the actions necessary for their fulfillment. These actions, sometimes pleasant, sometimes not, lead us to a state of being in which we remember that in giving, we receive. Shakti leads to the deepest fulfillment, where all paths begin and end.

By having distorted, culturally created ideals of what women or men should be, we confine Shakti to a heavenly "out there" state of idealized being that hides, and will eventually reveal, a demonized state. That which is unattainable is by nature incomplete and ultimately inhuman. The church's version of the Virgin Mary as a holy saint without sexuality and of Mary Magdalene as a prostitute are perfect examples of this idealization of the two rivers. Shakti brings us into our humanity fully, into our bodies fully, into relationship with all parts of ourselves fully.

All voices within our many-layered selves can be heard and expressed, felt and connected to through the free flow of Shakti. Bringing the lusty engagement for life of the black river and the love, purity, and serenity of the white river together heals the split in our femininity and masculinity. By expressing both, we can unite both in passionate, joyful, and loving embrace.

Magdalene is best known today for embodying the "pure" Divine Feminine, yet she is also cast as a dark, helpless, insignificant prostitute; two different views, both of which have some truth to them. This is because the Grail forms within us by uniting the pure white and lusty dark rivers of Shakti. These rivers of life force flow through each woman, creating and dissolving life.

The white river and the dark river are the sources of liking and disliking, attachment and aversion, pushing and pulling. These forces act on the mind each and every day, taking us away from our center of balance and equanimity. The white river impels us to like virtues, to be attracted to them, and to dislike that which we consider to be evil, negative, or bad for us—the dark river.

When we consider that what is good for us today may be bad for us tomorrow, and what is bad for us today may be the most beneficial thing for us tomorrow, we realize that staying attached to this ideal of righteousness actually makes us rigid. This type of thinking is what creates religions, leading to various forms of dogma and control, the most extreme being the Christian Inquisition, where thousands were massacred in the name of Christ.

Righteousness, or the desire for light to the exclusion of all else, leads to rejection of our own darkness and of lessons we might learn from matter and the subconscious. This misplaced rigidity has led to some of the greatest wars on our planet and the false notions of some religions being "better" than others. Love includes all in its embrace, regardless of what we are.

The dark river influences our mind in the opposite way. Our mind is constantly tossed between these two spiraling forces of manifestation, forcing us to remain caught in the maelstrom of our likes, dislikes, attachments, and aversions—what we think is right or wrong.

> *As my life had been focused in the river of light, there was not an awareness of the beauty and power of the dark river flowing just below the surface. It was only thought of or felt as the place of despair, grief, sadness, pain, and suffering. And it can grab hold, drowning you in those frequencies, and veil the well-kept secret and magic of its power to transmute and create. The discovery of the dark river, and merging it with the river of light in sacred marriage, opens one to the full and never-ending flow of Shakti in a pure and powerful way.* (C. O.)

The White River of Holy Desire: The Opener of the Way

Appreciation and gratitude are the openers of the white river, whose flow can be best called holy desire. When appreciation and gratitude are felt in the yoni, it becomes a holy portal to the universal womb. Flowing from the heart, appreciation and praise heal the yoni in a sanctified atmosphere, preparing the womb for sacred union that heals and blesses the man as much as it does the woman.

These upward-spiraling emotions of appreciation, gratitude, love, and compassion are natural feelings that form the basis of union. When they flow into your yoni from your sacred heart—or from your partner's heart—healing of old wounds can occur.

Holy desire is sexuality raised to a level of unconditional love and giving. Not just in lovemaking, but in the desire for the Divine in all parts of your life and relationships. Through this complete vulnerability you find yourself as love begins to master you. We give in order to give, not give in order to receive.

Holy desire is a wanting, an inner burning that propels you, fuels you to keep moving forward. Holy desire is passion to fulfill the soul's deepest yearning, passion to be all that you can be. Holy desire makes us give our all. Desire is the energy that makes all things grow, flower, and bloom. It enables the soul to expand and reach for the infinite and to surrender to the infinite, despite the fears that may arise. Holy desire never ends, as the universe is always expanding, as is the soul. The soul's desire for love can never be completely fulfilled. It is ongoing.

Holy desire is the beating heart of the soul; it is the life force of the soul, the soul's blood. Without this blood flowing through the soul's veins, we are lifeless, hollow. When the flow of desire is blocked, we start to die. When we forget our passions and allow them to fall by the wayside, then we lose a part of ourselves. The death of desire is the death of the soul, a death that only a profound shake-up can then reignite.

No matter how enlightened we become there is always more. In wanting more and stating it, we let God know that we want her. It is important to want God. Tell her so, every day. Holy desire is the life force, the golden thread that connects you and God. The more you amplify the voltage going through this thread, the more God will sit up and take notice and actually send you more.

Holy desire can be an intense force—sensual, powerful, and overwhelming. This is why many fear it; because once it is released you will not be able to control it, as it leads to the overflowing of the life force in you. When we live in holy desire we cannot be controlled, for we flow in life itself. We can, however, choose when to allow the tap of desire to be open, what effects and manifestations it will have, and how we choose to act on any wave of desire flowing through us.

Desire grows through intimacy, intimacy grows through desire. The more intimate we become with each other, the more we desire and want to know more and have more.

Be intimate with God; desire God. Redirect your desires toward this. Want God like a lover, deep inside you. Make love with God in this dance; show God your desire to be possessed by him or her. Always want more of God; let this be your prayer every day.

The Black River Speaks

I am your exhaustion, the heaviness, the fatigue of matter dragging you down. I am the entryway into the blackness, pulling you down deep, spiraling inward. I am the weight of matter, pulling you into form, into embodiment. I am the opposite of light, yet we work together to bring you into the here and now.

I am your resistance, the screams and cries of terror, the tears that have bound you into being a slave of the body. I am your sighs, the tiredness that overwhelms you, that keeps you inert. I am the grief and sorrow that keeps you stuck in your patterns. I am the body weighing down your soul, grinding you down until you sit and recognize me and my power. I am the energy within all matter, encoded within your bones, waiting to become crystalline by your surrender into my deep, dark well.

Sink into me. Fall down and spiral deep, losing your consciousness, gaining your freedom. Surrender to my embrace, the hug of matter, as we again become united.

Let your light descend. Enter the body; I will hold you and bring you real life. Allow yourself to become the heaviest you have ever been, and I will make you light again. I am the memory of the body, I am the memory held within the body, I am the memory that leads to your true Self once you have embraced and woven me into your life.

I am sloth, I am inertia; I am gravity, I am stability. I am your body. I make you solid and tangible. I am the sleep that hides within you until you contact me.

I am the perfect stability that supports Creation into being. I am the fluid silence of physical mastery. I am the glue of matter that binds atoms together. I am bondage, suffering, death, and inertia that you are too scared to face and acknowledge. I am part of life, and I signal the beginnings of new life. Enter death and you enter life.

I am the voice of your resentments, your loneliness, your feelings you have rationalized spiritually and intellectually. I am the voice that hides underneath your spiritual and political correctness. I am the root of your irritation with yourself.

I am the emptiness of your humanity, and I show you where you have betrayed your humanity. I am that which you have to dare to express, to take courage to share. I am the voice lurking in the shadows, waiting, festering for a moment to speak. I remind you of your glamorizations. I remind you of the human truth of relationship, not the white truth, but the grounded truth.

I show you your illusions and your fantasies that you design to keep you safe at night. I show you the falsity of your presence and what lies underneath it. I show you the real you, warts and all. I show you what you do not wish to see.

So honor me. Honor my voice within you. Keep the balance between your human needs and your divine giving. I ground your selflessness onto earth, into the body. Honor your body-world and its impulses. Do not let me take over, for if I do I will lead you into the deepest slumber and forgetting. I am the voice of matter trapped in light, and when honored I am the voice of Shakti released. I am the voice of the primal web of life, here and now relating on Earth.

So speak my name: scream it, whisper it, growl it, sing it. Love it all. My voice is your truth. Let me slip through your lips, just a droplet—a sigh, a soft moan—and flow with it, allow it, follow it back to my source. In this way you become the river. Breathe into whatever darkness arises, and breathe it out into expression. I am unearthing your shadow. All your grief, joy, primal rage—what are they all but flow? Soft eddies and vast waters, all of it is love. (W. C.)

When trapped in my embrace, you become steeped in ignorance, not even aware of my existence. You just go on fulfilling the mundane obligations of life, caught in their descending cycle, caught in a matrix. (P. A.)

BEGINNING THE JOURNEY

Great pathways of pain lie carved in the bodies of women, ages and ages of collective suffering are pressing closed the doorways to your own liberation. In forgetting the legacy of women's power, you have suffered the pain of being separated from parts of yourself you are no longer taught to honor and whose wisdom you no longer heed. The power is within you, and you are being called now to find and reclaim your inner divinity. To do this, you must first go into the darkness, discover all the ways you have repressed yourself and have been repressed, all the ways in which you have abandoned and forgotten your true nature. It is all stored in your body.

Your journey through the seven gates will take you into that darkness and will bring you back out into a clearer light. This is the gift that awaits: your greatest pain and your greatest freedom. Each of these gates has a voice to express. Each has its own nature and expression and each carries the pain and weight of having been separated from its own divinity.

Experiencing praise and pleasure, intertwined with ignorance, disrespect, mutilation, and pain at the first gate, entrance to the yoni, brought me into a deeper presence and appreciation with the "lips of love." The pulsing of the G-spot sent me swirling into the maelstrom of rape, violence, abuse, and misuse, with only a momentary memory of any acknowledgment or gratitude being expressed to me in the past. In the first touch of the third gate, the clitoris, the black rose in the dark river, a shiver of pleasure made way for the horror and pain of mutilation, molestation, and the numbness there that remains.

Yet I am re-membering—a raging river of darkness, hidden below the goodness, the peace, the beauty. My power, my fury, is not to be tempered. I will burn away all resistance, all hesitancy, and all memory that wants to control my flow. It is time. (C. O.)

The journey requires you to unite the light and dark rivers of Shakti. This deeply loving practice of opening the gates is an integral part of clearing the eighteen pathways. This culminates in the Shakti Circuit, which gathers all the energy to flow up the spine from the womb, through to the yoni, the perineum, the anus, the base of the spine, and then up through the interweaving currents of the spinal column into the Mouth of the Goddess.

In a woman's body, Shakti comes to life as the river of light emanating from the wellspring at the seventh gate deep within the womb. This river connects the womb to her true journey and sets her on the path that is the ever-spiraling flow of giving and receiving. So it manifests through women and men in a constant state of service, of giving in every moment, the giving that is simply being totally present and sharing of the Shakti flow out in every direction.

So women, by being able to access Shakti directly, find that in receiving from the Source they in turn are led to give. Men, however, access Shakti through the woman's form by first giving. Do you see the divine dance displaying itself once again? The woman in receiving, gives, the man in giving, receives. Only by reaching a place of conscious awareness to lead himself to the fifth gate in union with a woman will he access the true levels of Shakti that lie beyond it. In order to even access the fifth gate with a woman, his journey will already be one of openness, clarity, self-awareness, and giving. In giving, so he receives, and when they join in the deepest union at the fifth gate he can then journey with her to the sixth and seventh gates to experience the eternal wellspring that is held within her. (T. A.)

PROTECTING THE OPEN WOMB

What one takes in is through the web of life, and one can take in various energies and beings. In order for the womb to flower fully it is important that the man protect the womb opening so that the woman can become fully empathic and receptive. She may not have the ability to discern, to not hold back, as it is primarily her role to be open and giving. The man here has to act as the knight, the protector, dissolving any discarnate entities and thoughtforms that swarm to the womb's open magnetic and psychospiritual light fields, attracted to it in order to feed on it, and even to stop it from opening by doing so.

It is true that love needs no protection, and it is also important that the opening process is honored, allowed to flower and flourish. Like a flower the womb needs nurturing until it is fully grown, and then it can stand by itself and fend for itself. While it is in the process of flowering, especially in the third and fourth spirals, it is sensitive and needs the support, courage, valor, and noble selfless protection of the man in order for it to feel rooted and grounded in the sometimes delicate and unknown territories that it is venturing into in its opening process.

It is only through feeling safe on every dimension that the womb can fully flower by surrendering to its innate presence, which is initially delicate, unknown, untested, and uncharted.

This process is really living on the cutting edge of consciousness in the female form, as it is so little known about and discussed in today's world. To delve into the opening of the womb in the third and fourth spirals at this time on Earth is to be a pioneer into the unknown in many ways, yet this will soon change as the collective feminine consciousness reignites and flowers again, finding its true source of power and depth in the womb. This will flower again after 2012, as Earth comes back into alignment with Galactic Center, the Womb of the Galaxy, with much of the old paradigm being washed away and new ways (re)established based on the equality of male and female and mature consciousness.

After a few months of moving through the transition from the third spiral into the fourth, I began to notice when out in public how everyone was looking at me. Everywhere I looked I could see eyes upon me. Men and women of all ages and backgrounds would simply stare and openly look at my body and my face without turning away even when I gazed back. They seemed to be hypnotized.

I knew the face of love so well and yet it wasn't that face I was seeing. Their glances were mostly neutral yet with an intensity as if they could see and feel something unusual about me and were unable to divert their attention. They wanted something, either to absorb and feel for themselves, or they wanted to destroy and pull apart.

There was often a look of searching or incredible fascination, as I would walk with my husband through the streets. It was my husband who pointed this out to me, and once I began to look I could see that he was speaking the truth. If he had not been there I would have felt incredibly naked and vulnerable. I feel that had he not been there people would have approached me, stopped me in the street, and for sure sat with me in cafés and restaurants.

On a few occasions I noticed how women would look at me with spite and distrust, how they seemed to undress me with callous and suspicious eyes; again, my husband saw this too. Being so openhearted, I could not change anything about my being or way in the world. It was impossible to close my heart and walk with an air of protection or power. Yes there was power there, but it was the power of love merged with the power of extension to all, and especially toward those who were being pulled, drawn by my essence.

I now know with hindsight that it would have been neglectful and irresponsible to be without protection during those days. As a woman I ask you to take on that responsibility that your womb, your heart, and your overall countenance will attract, draw, and pull toward you many people. Do not place yourself in situations or environments that do not feel supportive or secure. Avoid people that you know are draining and demanding. You must treat yourself as an innocent child as this light of divinity begins to grow within you. Communicate with your partner, explain what is happening, and allow him to see for himself the evidence of this magnetism. He will immediately feel the rising up of his instinctual protection for you, and you will need this.

It's very different from sexual attraction. It is not that. I would even say that it's stronger and even more out of control than a magnetism between a man and a woman. When within this journey, it will be impossible to harden and close yourself off. And why would you shorten this journey or cut short its flowering? My husband created a force field around us that kept people at bay and respectful of our space. They were still able to look and draw from me what they needed for their healing. But it was at levels and distances that were safe for all parties. (A. A.)

THE MANIFESTATION OF A NEW WORLD THROUGH PASSION AND DETACHMENT

Using and understanding primal, instinctual, dynamic forces in harness with the male forces of order, detachment, and reason leads to a dynamic equality between male and female that has the power necessary to create and manifest a new world. The wisdom required here is of detachment and sensitivity in being able to navigate and establish a bridge between the lower and higher self, so that the lower self may be harnessed by the higher self.

Passion and detachment go hand in hand. Passion, overflowing joy, and exuberant dynamic love without detachment means one can get lost in lust and the animal side of the instinctual urges. Detachment refines the fire of passion and the primordial urge for life into clarity, discernment, and contained power when it is required, and wild joy when that is required. Prayer, meditation, and peace serve as counterpoints to fire and Shakti. Being alone, having time to reflect and gather the strands of life that creative passion stirs, allows the next level of awareness and creation to manifest and even more life juice to flow, juice that supports light force and deeper peace . . . and so the wheel turns.

7
The Web of Life

The Connecting of Intuitive Songlines

The third spiral is when we enter and deepen into the web of life. The web of life is a pulsing, breathing envelope of Shakti that connects all living beings on Earth from animals to humans, plants to trees to stars and beyond. The web networks together all life-forms without discrimination. It works through our etheric bodies, connecting through our auric fields to all other life-forms.

The web and its songlines are how we stay in tune with the environment and each other on an intuitive level as through the web we can sense what is happening in the flow of life force even many miles away.* The ways to tap in to this intuitive understanding are well known to animals and indigenous societies worldwide.

The web is different from the light grids that surround our planet in that it is the life force that supports the grids, not just on this planet but all planets. The web has always been here and will never go away. Our connection to it has been disrupted over time, resulting in the current ecological crisis on Earth and separation from feminine wisdom.

We stay connected to the web of life through acts of offering, giving,

*This is similarly discussed in my book *The Power of Shakti,* pages 178–81.

service, and gratitude. Offering to the web of life all of what you have makes sacred who you are. It feeds the web, and the web in turn feeds you. The web is in a state of perpetual creating, undulating, pulsing. It is as alive as you and me, and infinitely intelligent. In actively supporting life-giving energies or acts of procreation, we can tune in to the web of life and allow it to guide us. In the initial experience of connecting to the web you can literally lose your small self's sense of identity, immersing into this pulse that is behind all life.

The web of life connects all dimensions and is anchored on Earth in the womb of the world. Webs are nonhierarchical, nonpatriarchal; they are cooperative in nature, which is how they connect us to Earth and beyond. It is this web that has throughout history furnished humanity with information that has led to leaps in our spiritual evolution.

Working with the web of life allows one to be completely present with the energies of the earth and to thereby gain access to many other dimensions. In the past this connection was done through sound and ritual. It is through this connection that we become aware of our environment and merge with it. And by connecting to it we heal and align ourselves to the natural rhythms and motions of life. We connect to the web of life by offering and giving ourselves to it. When we do so, we are taken into the oneness that all life shares. The "I" becomes lost in the one that connects our hearts.

The web can be seen as a glowing silver-white web, threading, weaving, and sustaining harmony in all things. Your body, your flesh, your nerves, your cells, and your very being are permeated by this web. Offering ourselves sincerely to the web allows us access. Giving something that is important to us directly to the earth—our energy, our desires, our sincere heartfelt prayers and gratitude—rather than just taking (particularly at sacred sites) allows us conscious access. In the offering we receive and become the conduit, the circuit that is in constant flow, receiving and giving through the open heart of gratitude.

Initially the best way to do this practice is while visiting a sacred site in nature, where you feel resonance, where you feel at home. Sit down at twilight (or at night if the moon is visible), in a place near some trees and away from city lights, city noise, and interference, if possible.

Connecting to the Web of Life

1. Take off your shoes and sit barefoot on the earth. Focus on your heart. Breathe. Now focus on your feet and the field of energy that extends down from the feet into the earth. Visualize it.
2. Breathe down through the soles of your feet into this field. Push down the breath, and visualize the field extending.
3. Now extend this field of energy from your feet into Gaia downward; deep down. Allow yourself to plunge down, through the soil, through the many layers of rock, earth, and fire, into the womb of the earth. This is a vast, black, all-enveloping space. Sit here for a moment.
4. Now ask, and pray to Mother Gaia, in your own words, from your own heart, to feel and extend your connection to her. Offer her yourself, offer her your service, and thank her for being your foundation, your anchor, your home. Breathe into this connection, connecting heart, womb, feet, to Gaia. Feel this space within you. For it is part of you, and you are part of it, as part of your origins, your roots, and your foundation.
5. Now open your eyes, and focus on a tree or a group of trees. Soften your gaze until it becomes slightly blurry. Start to see the aura of the tree, the energy field surrounding it. Be patient. Follow the field of the tree in its expansion outward. See or visualize a silver-white thread or web extending outward and upward to the moon. Look up to the moon, and feel your feet.

   Welcome to the web of life.

In the Native American tradition, Grandmother Spider spins the web of life. From within her belly she spins her web outward, creating the worlds. If we were to feel ourselves as Grandmother Spider, we realize we too can spin webs from our wombs, attracting all we need to us.

We do not lack anything, and we have all we need to create and manifest a home, good relationships, and our soul's purpose.

When the time comes to move on from one cycle of time or period of manifestation, like Grandmother Spider we can simply draw all the cords and web connections back into our womb and move on to another location, to then weave again the web of life and connection.

We all hold the power to weave ourselves into the web of life, to bring us all we need to be abundant, sustained, and connected. However, for many of you there has been a break, a partial severing stemming from forgetfulness of your connection to the radiant web of life. You have forgotten how to weave this web as it has been obscured by the wounds and hurts you carry in the womb. Now, remember.

GAIA: WOMB OF THE WORLD AND GATEWAY TO THE DIVINE

The womb is the center of a woman's power. It is the generator of light, power, and joy, the keeper, bearer, and sustainer of life. Through her womb and the Alta Major chakra, or mouth of the goddess, situated at the back of the neck, she becomes receptive to the currents of life that move and sustain creation.

The Womb of the World is the heart of Gaia's creative force, the womb deep in the earth from where Gaia gives birth to new creations and from where all truly transformative births occur that influence and shift human consciousness. It is from the Womb of the World that Gaia, and the lineage of ancient mothers past, present, and future, give their sanction and blessing to all those who wish to help humanity through the feminine.

Anyone throughout history who has transformed the planet's consciousness in any major way has gone through the Womb of the World, or been assisted by midwives who have this connection.

She is the power of woman, not afraid to show or use it, yet at the same time is elegant. She holds both sides of the feminine in equal measure; the power of woman throughout the ages embodied in the now.

She empowers women to embrace and celebrate their feminine power; to know their role as women and their importance and equality in a patriarchal age. Her uninhibited nature allows her to express the truth of all women without reservation.

She is the teacher of the secrets of the earth, the need for women to claim their true sexuality and body as a source of power and as a bridge to the divine. Unafraid of her sexual power, independence, fertility, and magnetism, she reveals and initiates others into the mystery, joy, and unlimited potential of divine co-creation. She teaches how to access and open the womb through sacred rites, ceremony, sound, breath, and specific practices. She is the gatekeeper and midwife to the primordial Womb of the World, knowing its importance in birthing new realities and manifesting heaven on earth.

A midwife guides the birthing process, holding the space for the womb to birth its creation, guiding the descent of spirit into form, assisting the mother to open, let go, give her creation to the world, and feel comforted that another is there who knows the process and whom she can rely on. She opens the way, becoming the feminine pillar of strength and care that allows the physical mother of the birthing process to focus on her task alone.

She acts as an interface between the divine thoughtforms and ideas held in the Divine Mind and Womb and their earthly manifestation. This web of light, held within the earth's womb, the trees, nature, and the moon, is also reflected in the ley lines that connect and crisscross the planet. Working with the web of light, one is allowed to be completely present with the energies of the earth, and in doing so one accesses many other dimensions beyond just this Earth.

A MIRROR: LIFE IN THE WOMB/LIFE IN THE WORLD

Your human life was formed and created while you were in your mother's womb. The forming and fashioning of your soul happened in the unfolding of the spark of life when it was in the Galactic Center, or Divine Mother's womb. You replicate the inner conditions of the human womb and your journey through it, in your lived external lives as adults. You replicate the inner conditions of the Galactic Womb and your journey through it in your authentic return to soul as a true adult.

All the hang-ups, the obstacles, the drives, the attributes that you have as an "adult" came from the human womb. All the soulful attributes that you have as an "adult" came from the Galactic Womb, the fashioning center and origin of the soul. All the external circumstances, movements, blocks, and instinctual gut-driven attributes that make up who you are, and the way you think in the world, arose from the womb and now guide you. You are in effect creating the womb outside of you or still living in the womb, each day of your life, until you understand your birth traumas and lessons and heal them.

Your birth determines your whole life. How you are born, and how you choose to incarnate, creates the course of fate for your whole life. Yet this is not fate; this can be easily determined by looking closely at your birthing process. Imagine how your mother felt, how you felt within her as your heart, your limbs, and your brain slowly formed under the guiding and animating force of the soul, the divine spark of life. And how she felt as your body was maturing and ripening within hers, and all the feelings, thoughts, and influences that were flooding you from her.

What was being exchanged, and who was doing what to the other? Were you one? What was uniquely yours and was forming just for you? How did she influence your choices and movements, and what was just your own choice?

And then comes the ultimate journey of birth and death, from womb to vagina to this world, from darkness into the light, the same journey in reverse that you take when you die and leave the body, down a long tunnel back into the light. From darkness arises all light. The very word *Guru* also means bringing darkness into light.

And all of this is remade when you return to the Galactic Womb or Galactic Center and become reborn, when time stops and "rewinds" itself back to the moment of conception, of original innocence, when it was all being first created.

Imagine how the Divine Mother felt as your soul formed from nothingness, from the first Pulse of Creation. As your monad, your different layers of energy bodies, your sheer uniqueness as a soul never separate from her arose, what were the choices you made here to do in this incarnation, and what did you choose to master and learn? What was the toughest thing you willingly agreed to?

Each of these journeys, with their obstacles, its length of time in labor and dying, the preverbal emotions you go through, and your responses to the journey, indicate who and what you are, and what you still have not yet completed, learned, or given.

In human birth these responses form much of your preverbal programming that then dictates the course of your life until you become conscious of them and reprogram them, or completely dissolve them. To do this is to literally rewrite your life, its flow and your destiny. You become reborn by deleting old programming that has you captive, captive precisely because you have forgotten about it, as it happened when you were in the womb before you had thoughts and feelings as you know them now.

But you did have a soul then, and that is where these deep impressions and beliefs are lodged and stored, playing out as the undercurrent of your thoughts and feelings, the hidden structure of how and what you think, the directions your subconscious urges take you, and the beliefs that are inviolable.

This may be hard to fathom. But have you ever wondered what happened in your mother's womb as you were growing? Have you talked to her about your birth, the labor time, how she felt? Have you asked her what the pregnancy was like in detail? Have you delved so deep back into your memory of when you were in the womb or even before birth? Do you recognize what it is you were feeling and what was happening to you?

In India it is said that the whole of a person's karma is created in the womb and your journey out of it. Other yogis share that this journey is one of seven ways in which we create and reveal our karma. Whichever way we look at it, our gestation within the mother's womb, our first birth, with all its feelings, cues, responses and external influences both negative and positive, and then our journey away from it through the vagina and into this world, create a major part of us that absolutely has to be looked at, addressed, and healed. If not, it will forever dominate your subconscious and create a timeline and lifeline of an artificial and limiting nature, stopping you from taking your second birth of the spirit.

You have to be free from your first, flesh birth to be reborn into innocence, your birth into Spirit.

BIRTHING INTO SPIRIT

Reprogramming your lifeline through Rebirthing Breathwork, Holotropic Breathwork, Four Baskets Healing, deep inquiry, hypnosis, and remembrance of the decisions and preverbal memories that you carry within is essential for you to become your authentic self that is free and able to move clearly in life to reach your highest potential. Many peoples' deepest blocks are inaccessible until they delve deep in to this place, and every human being has part of their soul and personality structure mapped out in their birth journeys, be it the human birth journey or the stellar birth journey.

These structures, when seen and dissolved, enable you to become an adult and to be born of the spirit, free of the flesh.

The Four Baskets

When you are born, there are four stages to your emerging out from the womb into this world. These four stages of growth that all humans journey through become four underlying psychological and behavior patterns of how you act, feel, and think throughout your whole life. Until you have resolved them, you are still a child waiting to become an adult.

These four baskets, or four stages, of the birth journey are the different phases by which the fetus develops as it travels throughout the labor process into this world. These four are lived experiences and wounds that design much of who and what we are. Your whole life is influenced by the choices and decisions about how to be in life that come forth from these nine months. Understanding, addressing, and dissolving many of these decisions and patterns of behavior provide answers to deep-seated and nagging questions like "Why does this happen?" and "Why do I act like this?"

These deep programs keep you bound, running your life like a tape continuously repeating itself in a feedback loop, keeping you stuck in the same pattern over and over again. To know these underlying wounds are there is the first step. For them to be healed and dissolved is the next.

Your lifeline, deathline, and birthline all change when the four baskets are healed. It is like an underlying pattern or cause gets seen and wiped out. Depending on which stage or basket you are in, and how much energy and effort you put into the task, it can happen quite quickly. The key is to approach it on many levels, both with breath, inquiry, light, and womb healing all working together.

The First Basket

As labor commences, and as the fetus moves, it starts to feel tired, wanting to come out but not able to, and this creates a feeling of helplessness and frustration. The baby cannot do anything. It is being subjected to a lot of changes, expansions, and contractions in the womb. The walls close in with great discomfort and tightness, and it would like to come out but nothing is possible. There is no way out.

A first basket person has no drive, no motivation, and little to no life force in achieving anything in life. They have no real energy or joy and have little faith in themselves or in life in general. They have feelings of no progress, inertness, lethargy, and sloth, sitting here but not actually being here. Everything is happening around them but not to them.

"Why am I here?" is the question of the static first-basket person. They never finish projects, giving up halfway through: nothing gets completed as too many obstacles, resistances, and failures happen. They simply become overwhelmed by the unfairness of life and think life has it in for them. They can actually feel this force of resistance against them, conniving against them in a wall of resistance to all they try to do, be it in events, circumstances, environments, or people.

Bad luck is a constant. Rejections and failures are the norm; they never pass the grade and never get the job. They have low self-esteem, feeling guilty and shameful for their sloth, and never realize what it is they are trying to break down. They never want to raise up their head for fear of it being pushed back down again. Life is a cruel, hard place, and God is a cruel, hard being for the first-basket person, who often resorts to drink and drugs to mask powerlessness. Guilt and shame are also prevalent.

The Second Basket

The womb has become unbearable now in the second phase of birthing. As the baby struggles anxiously to come out, it is being pushed in and out, back and forth toward its feeling of freedom. Then delivery begins! There is hope. Now I can come out, there is the sense of "I can do something," but still, it will not happen.

Somebody who is stuck in the second basket feels helpless. In taking up a career and in relationships they are stuck, not feeling that they get the love or attention they want, but they just do not know how to express or attain it, as it gets stuck within them. Everything is middle of the line, middle of the road, average, the same as everyone else. They do not really want or wish for anything else and will settle with what they have or what they are told to do.

Desperation, depression, anxiety, going to extremes, claustrophobia, the need to escape and run away are often seen in people stuck in this basket. Worthlessness and sloth may also dominate, although they can get roused and fired up by something that really grabs them, although they may never finish such a thing. They may also have a lack of concentration and have the feeling that little can happen to or for them. They might want to leave anything and everything and get irritated about little things. The second-basket person puts in 100 percent effort and receives back 30 percent.

The Third Basket

The third-basket baby can see the light at the end of the womb and moves purposefully toward it. "I will get there" is its mantra. It is inevitable, and even if you feel resistance, even if you feel a "no," it will not dissuade you. You will try and try again because you *know* you will make it. "No" means nothing, resistance is futile as you *will* move through all resistance with certainty and determination.

The third basket person will have to perform good efforts to get something in life. They work hard and consistently in any field to achieve moderate success, but they will get it. They make great students, as they pay attention and feel as though he/she understands and receives. They may not be the most talented, but whatever talent they possess they will maximize to its fullest, and market themselves well. They are hard workers, and ones that any boss is happy with. If they are their own boss, they will be their own greatest critic and will push themselves consistently. They make progress, will be expecting fruits, but are not able to reap the fruits fully. For 100 percent effort they make 60 percent gain.

The Fourth Basket

This is the way into freedom, by actually coming out of the womb in grace and ease. These births are simple, straightforward, and easeful, with natural birthing practices usually employed. There is little struggle, and labor is fast. One friend of mine went into labor in a hospital in the morning and was drinking a cup of tea three hours later with her parents in a coffee shop, swaddled baby under arm!

These fourth-basket people often experience success easily. All good things come to them relatively effortlessly. People and resources are attracted to them and want to help them. They get what they want by itself and are asked and approached for things. Grace, ease of life and attraction, the "Midas touch" are the characteristics of the fourth-basket person. "I have" is its mantra. Soul purpose becomes manifested and attracted to you from an early age. You live the law of attraction without doing anything at all. It is, in fact, given to you.

When you are reborn in this way, after moving through and healing the other baskets, it is very tangible, and a lot shifts quite quickly in your life, as the underlying resistance is gone. A new pattern reveals itself, and the old navigation guidelines, charts, maps, and tools become obsolete. In this transition period, it is best to wait and see what arises rather than force anything, as grace now dictates your life and will give you much more than what you thought possible before as you make the jump from one basket stage to the next.

Reaching the fourth basket, moving through all the other baskets, requires that you examine and let go of all beliefs. That is the journey. The belief that anyone needs anything is just that: a belief. This is painful and can be felt at times in the body, which tries to validate the mind's reality that it is real and true. Bodymind are one, but it is all controlled by the mind. Once you know this, you become self-responsible and apply this in every situation.

You need nothing. All the things you feel you need, cry out for, yearn for, are beliefs. The actions that make you react unlovingly, escape, or react are also beliefs. They can never be healed, only seen, owned, dismantled, and emptied out in your actions. If you feel you need anything, that is merely the mind's reality and a belief.

You need nothing. Nothing makes you whole. Wholeness is when there is nothing left to need, want, or attach to. All is present, and nothing is out of the moment now.

Of course, you need home, food, and shelter. That is not what we are sharing. We are talking about how the mind controls your reality through beliefs that run like an undercurrent through your thinking and emotions. These beliefs stop you from love and from experiencing love as there is always a compare-and-contrast button in any and every belief system. With your set of love beliefs you think, "If this does not measure up to that, then it is not love," or you come up with a similar method of judging

Beliefs about how things are or should be are pervasive and subtle. Love should be like this, look like this, be like how it was with others, be like how it is written in books, for instance. Love is much more than that and expresses itself uniquely for each person. Love has depth, strength. It is the most powerful force in the universe. It can stop people dead in their tracks, it can change worlds in one moment, it can expose beliefs and wounds in one second. It stands by, and works through, light and dark, it weaves its way through all light and all dark and is the only quality that does so. Love has no reason to it. It goes beyond reason, right or wrong, and love, my friends, is insane.

It can never be sane to the conditioned mind, as it breaks all laws, busts all boundaries, and cracks open any and all beliefs about what it is, or should be, once it is experienced. Even the expectation of what love should feel like has to go in order for it to be accepted.

You are part of God. God does not look outside for help, for something to pray to. It rests and abides within itself and sees what is true or not. It neither needs nor grasps, wants nor attaches, but calmly abides within itself. It then enjoys itself in the play of love.

What stops this are beliefs, engrams, structures of belief, and rigidified thoughtforms that have been repeated over many years, even lifetimes, to create grooves in the brain. These grooves then guide all incoming energy, emotion, and thought into these patterns, defining your behavior, responses, and reactions. The only way out is to identify the groove and dissolve it, bringing it back into its original, unformed, or smooth state: innocence.

To realize innocence is to be reborn of Spirit, moving beyond the first birth of the flesh. This takes complete self-responsibility. By assuming the kingly mantle of total responsibility, one realizes God, and lives in love. Nothing is outside, and nothing causes you to react in an unloving way, as you *know* it is you.

This world is made for your reflection. The world is you. You are the world, and all the relations you have are also you. You are everywhere. There is nowhere you are not. Can you handle that? Everything you feel, everything you react against, all your relations, mirror part of you. In fact, you can say this world was created by you, for you, for your own growth, and eventually your own amusement and joy.

Taking complete responsibility means taking responsibility for the soul, the spirit, those around you, and eventually the world. This does not have to be a loud, overt, screaming out to the rooftops action. It can be quiet, and equally as effective. To be responsible for those around you does not mean you take away their responsibility and render them weak and dependent. No.

To be responsible for those around you means that you ask them to also realize they have no holes, graspings, attachments, and needs, and that they too are self-responsible. And yet you still take on that responsibility, to point out truth to them with love, penetrating them deeply, yet with softness. Then the purpose of all relationship, previously based on need, becomes clear. The purpose of all relationship is simply to share and give love, for in loving another you are but loving yourself—divine selfishness. You constantly are making the One Self feel love and feel good, the One Self that you and all others share. If you are feeling it, then so are others in some way. And yet, you are still alone and content by yourself.

As the Brhadaranyaka Upanishad puts it, "It is not for the sake of the husband that he is loved, but for one's own sake that he is loved. It is not for the sake of the wife that she is loved, but for one's own sake that she is loved. It is not for the sake of the sons that they are loved, but for one's own sake that they are loved. It is not for the sake of all that all is loved, but for one's own sake that all is loved. The Self, my dear, should be Realized, and it is through hearing, reflection and meditation that Self, and all, is known . . ."

Emptiness goes hand in hand with self-responsibility. Together they lead to truth, dissolving or "healing" all things, all parts of self. All denial gets embraced. All judgments become forgiven, let go of, and laughed at. All abandonment gets reunited, all isolation becomes surrendered, all betrayal becomes trust, faith, and knowing.

LIVING FROM THE WOMB-HEART

To live in the third spiral means that your center has dropped completely into the womb-heart, and you are living from this space. Dropping your sense of reaction and response down into the womb is a much more silent, still place than the ever-active mind.

Become aware of which center you are speaking from, thinking from, feeling from. Do you feel it from the mind, or do you feel it from the heart? Or are you feeling it from the heart and mind united? Be aware of this every day. The more you are simply aware of this, the more your attention can descend down into the quiet, still, peaceful strength of the womb.

To do this requires focusing on your heart, and your belly, with both your hands and breath for five minutes each day. Try this now.

Connecting with the Womb-Heart

1. Place one hand over the heart and one over the womb. These are a woman's two hearts.
2. Feel a figure eight of gold light connecting your two hearts. It will give you a quiet strength when you feel caught in suffering or despair, or when you simply need to go within.
3. Now, breathe gently into your womb. Sound the Aramaic (the language of Christ and Mary) sound *Meleet. Me* on the in breath, *leet* on the out breath. *Meleet* means "completeness, fullness," the complete circle of the womb.
4. Now breathe gently into your heart. Sound the Aramaic word *Min-Beesha. Min* on the in breath, *Beesha* on the out breath.

Min-Beesha means "ripeness, fruition," as when a ripe fig or apple is blooming, ready to be plucked and eaten fresh from the tree, full of goodness, bursting with juiciness, vitality, and life force.

5. Now, sound them both together . . . *Meleet Min-Beesha.*
6. Connect them both with the breath and in the infinity or figure eight loop.

Eventually, you will feel a beat in your second hand echoing the heart-beat in your first hand.

> *When I experienced the womb-heart breathing, with the Aramaic toning of "Meleet Min-Beesha," I felt my heart and womb merge together. The inner landscape revealed to me two giant transmitting pyramids of power, the womb and the heart being pulled together by the sonic sounds.* Meleet *drew my heart down, while* Min Beesha *drew my womb up.*
>
> *As the two pyramids faced each other, there was a contraction, hesitancy, and a moment to savor. . . . I was about to merge these two enormous power stations. What would happen when Shakti met Bhakti?*
>
> *I continued the breath and the toning, and as the apex of the pyramids began to penetrate each other I experienced glorious shafts of light and creation being born into this world. It was as if they were waiting all along to come together. Duality dissolved with the emergence of a True Authentic Woman. The key is the reunion of the open womb with the full heart. (A. A.)*

COMPLETE IMMERSION: THE BRIDGE TO FULL EMPOWERMENT

The collected memories of the feminine are stored in the womb as thoughtforms that need clearing by each one who enters, leaves, and serves this space. The history of woman is here; the abuses, the empowerment, and the healing—also your abuses, your empowerments, your healing.

In the womb one plunges into the feminine ocean. The womb

guards death, the biggest hole in the psyche, the greatest thing we avoid. The hole in your being, the loneliness of the gap, the absence felt within you, is the avoidance of death. Your fear and avoidance of death create a gap in awareness that creates a longing in the heart; this gap is the seed of all fear, and its dissolving also.

Around this hole is where personality is structured, the core of the ego that guards death and time. To become aware of your biggest secret, death, and this hole, is the dying of your fear. When the debris and pattering from your cells are cleared out through its arising to the surface, then the womb can realign to its new blueprint. This residue as decay within the body and womb *has* to be released for full ascension to happen. It is not enough to release it merely from the bodymind.

The experience of void and the womb is the start of the development and remembrance of your true nature and the stepping out of the world of fear. If a person can experience space, then their true nature will arise spontaneously.

If you really aspire to be transformed, to be a light unto yourself, then the first act is of total immersion and totality in this quest. Do not do things in half steps; if you want to do something, do it the whole way. Only totality transforms. Only at full intensity can you transmute from the ordinary to the extraordinary.

If you feel miserable stay with it; experience it fully. Do not escape it in any way, as you are denying yourself a truth. Simply be with it; be grateful for it no matter what occurs. Turn it into meditation. In staying with the feeling and intensity with no judgment on the situation, the pain will spread. Allow it to run through; it is cleansing and preparing you for the sweetness of the Black Light. Accept it, welcome it, be grateful.

When you accept the pain and suffering with no judgment on what it is, in humility and with patience, the energy instantly begins to transform. Whenever anything is total, it transforms into its opposite. Your suffering now becomes your portal of initiation, your blessing, your doorway to your heart's desire. Now it is a time of remembering.

In the third spiral, one faces a turning point; of life and death, of death to the old identity of you, and new life to a new you that is free and innocent of the conditionings, expectations, and bondage of the old you. The path of eternal life is very much one of death; progressive and successive deaths. Each death is a rebirth.

Death reminds you that you are mortal, reminding you to get up and experience life now. With death on your shoulder, one cannot ignore life and what it presents you with any longer. Absence reminds you of the amazing potential for total presence; this is what the best spiritual teachers do: reveal their absence to facilitate you into presence, or bewilderment as the case may be!

The third spiral holds life and death in each hand. It holds a space for life to reveal, create, and generate itself, and holds a space for death, to conceal, dismantle, clothe, and dissolve forms and ideas. This is found by holding your breath between your inhale and exhale. When you do this for long enough you experience this point between life and death and the fear that lies here also.

This is dangerous, radical, holy, and sacred—the bridge to full empowerment.

The Black Egg Practice

1. Slow down, sit down, and enter a quiet space.
2. Imagine your own mother standing in front of you. Say this to her once you are still:

   "You have always looked after me. Because you endure all the hardships of illness, pain, sorrow, and fear, because you fed me, clothed me, cleaned me, and loved me, I am now alive to become enlightened. From time without beginning, each and every being has been a mother to me, like you, my present mother. You all help me. Let me help you."
3. Bring to mind the suffering you have seen your mother face—physical, emotional, mental. See it in her as she is standing in front of you.

4. Now picture all of it as dense black smoke.
5. Breathe it deep into your heart. *Feel it.*
6. It is black, solid, hot, heavy—the texture of poison.
7. Inhale and exhale it now through all the pores of your body; each and every cell, while reciting the following:

   "I take in myself all the different sufferings of my mother to purify and heal.

   "I bring this forth to me, I bring this forth to me, I bring this forth to me.

   "*I am I am I am.*"
8. See this blackness in your heart as a black egg. Draw in the black smoke and its causes, and dissolve into the blackness in your own heart. As you draw it in, thank her three times for giving you life.
9. Release all smoke, and all feelings, from your bodymind and heart.
10. Breathe out cool white light from the heart.
11. Feel it opening up space.
12. *Now, breathe black in and white out.*

Offer yourself, your body, your wealth, your virtue, your unique gifts, so that the Mother can be clearer in body, speech, and mind. Give all of yourself to receive it all.

THE IMPORTANCE OF GRATITUDE AND BEAUTY

We have spoken earlier of the importance of experiencing gratitude as we move forward in this journey. In gratitude, we realize that we cannot get love, we can only receive it, and we can only fully receive it by giving it away. To have all, give all. In this we realize that there is no source by which to get love; there is only the choice to abide in gratitude and extend love.

To choose kindness is to choose gratitude, as it shows that you value the kindness that you have been given in order to exist, and even have the blessing of having a body. God has extended the kindness to you, and now to receive more of this kindness we have to give it away in action to our fellow beings.

To be truly happy is to live in gratitude. Living in gratitude and in grace means accepting whatever comes one's way, both "good and bad," with thankfulness. There is no exception to what one can be thankful for, as gratitude wears down our resistance to conflicts, humbles us, and brings us into joy and oneness as we start to see that if we thank and bless all things in our life, we enter a state of peace with kindness to all.

The knowledge that we can die any moment, and that death is our ally, teacher, and friend, leads to deeper appreciation and gratitude. In the blessing of this moment of life as we have it today, in the conflict that arises, in the "unfortunate" circumstances that happen, there is a lesson for our soul that we have created in order to find the peace of the open, giving heart as it blesses and receives all things equally through the focus of gratitude and appreciation. This heart makes all things full by thanking it, emptying it of any resentment, frustration, or thoughts of harm.

This leads to beauty. Beauty results from one's perception and not just from the person, place, object, or emotion perceived. Beauty arises from the clarity of our own perception. What we often describe as beautiful is an interpretation, one that has been taught to us, a perception that one thing is beautiful and another is ugly. To see beauty is to see things as they are and to appreciate something simply for what it is, for its purpose in Creation, and how it fits into the whole scheme of life. In seeing beauty, we see beyond the conditioned senses and see the life force, the shimmering light, in all life.

To see beauty we see with the heart and connect to what we are seeing and communicating with through the heart. When we truly see reality it is beautiful as it involves no judgment, no naming or identifying with things, no past history or conditioning. We see in the present moment, with empty mind and open heart.

This reality can be experienced through the senses only when the mind stops interpreting what it is experiencing. For the mind constantly gives a commentary on everything that with which it comes into contact, avoiding the direct experience of what actually *is;* therefore we cannot experience directly what is. Without the mind's interpretation and commentary, we can see the beauty in the rotting pile of dung lying on the street as everything becomes a reflection of what you think yourself to be. If you have no judgment about the value of something as opposed to the value of something else, then you can appreciate the nature and utility of all things.

In true beauty we do not exclude anything but embrace everything as living reflections of our nature, reflections that serve a vital purpose to show us where our mind still judges and misunderstands. Heaven is not somewhere else; it is right here in this perception. Beauty is not about how a person, place, object, or emotion looks or feels; it is about how you, the one who is looking, feels. The beauty that we experience out there is a direct reflection of the beauty of what is happening inside you. When you are in a state of joy and feel uplifted everything appears beautiful to you on the outside. This feeling naturally leads us toward being kind and extending this kindness and beauty to others in tender, receptive presence, leading to harmlessness.

For those who wish to embody this reality, you will go through a stage of being the "vessels of sweet sorrow," of empathy and compassion, the ones on the planet who cry to relieve the sufferings of others, feeling their sadness, pain, and distress. Here, we do not cry for ourselves but for everyone as a service to humanity in order to release them. When we cry these tears to relieve the sufferings of others, we also get transformed by feeling the pain of the whole world.

PART FOUR

The Womb of Gaia and Its Guardians

8
Transcending the Self

The Mystic's Path

Ripe are those who from their inner wombs birth ardor; they shall feel a breath from the heart of the universe.

The fourth spiral of the womb opens when one enters the Womb of the World, the Womb of Gaia, and encounters its guardians. This is where you face the collective shadow realms, where you discover the deepest fragments of the womb-soul self that has been lost and is now refound. These are the places where you have split off from loving parts of your shadow and soul and have left the feminine essence of love.

In the fourth spiral of the womb we meet head-on the fear of death, the fear of the void, the emptiness, from which we come in perfection, and to which we all inevitably return. Within this spiral lies your biggest lesson, the shadow and pattern that have dogged you for many lifetimes. When you meet this fully, it can lead to feelings of deep struggle as your soul presence merges with your human presence, and parts of you literally get deleted, emptied out, in this merging of womb-heart-soul. This is the biggest burning of suffering that enables you to bathe in the light. It is like the carrying of your own personal cross, the burden of ages, now lifted.

We enter the fourth spiral through a different doorway from those used to access the other spirals of the womb. This is a mystical journey and can only be accessed through the mystic's path. There is no rational explanation or way to access this space from where life arises, except through surrender and the experiential practices of Womb Diving, Womb Breathing, and merging with the Womb of Gaia at womb sites around the world. Perhaps the greatest way to experience it fully, without compromise, on all levels, is merging with the beloved in sacred union.

SACRED RELATIONSHIP

As self-identity and illusion dissolve and the truth of "no self" arises, one dies to the self and becomes reborn, leaving the womb. One graduates from being a child, a teenager, into an adult and beyond into awakening. The path of Womb Wisdom points toward this being a journey that two beings can take together in sacred relationship, although it can be taken alone as well, and in essence it is taken alone even by these two beings walking together hand in hand.

The greatest obstacles to sacred union are the idea of an *I* and need. Need is what fuels the *I*—need for another, need to fill the hole in yourself, need to get something you think you do not have from another. This is what drives relationship as most relationships are based on need and are therefore not unconditional. This need also extends to being right and to retaliation out of a need to protect one's self. But love needs no protection. love can never be harmed.

The idea of a self or *I* prevents union, as two *I*'s can never unite. From this basis of letting go of the self, sacred union can occur within you and with another body. To make sacred is to sanctify, give away, and dissolve the *I*. Union is when there is not two. It is only when there is no self to be aware of that union automatically occurs.

Very few people are aware of this as they constantly wish to unite their *I*'s in some kind of idea that this is sacred. This only leads to conflict, unhappiness, and suffering as all suffering arises from the idea of there being an *I*. Die to the *I* and Union will manifest.

The question to ask is, "Would this conflict/drama/suffering be happening if there was no *I* here now?" Then realign to this truth. If both people follow this, then there will be no conflict, merely laughter. Sounds simple, doesn't it?

It is, but to remember it in the heat of emotions, which are again fuel for attachment to the dream state, is another thing. But just to remember it once, gently and listening to this wisdom, can defuse the clamor, denial, stubbornness, and ridiculousness of the *I*.

Sacred union can be seen as a powerful and relentless process upon which the realization of nothingness is magnified and quickened. The "other" will be sure to highlight all the aspects of your remaining self that are still formed, unmoving, and rigid. Without the other you could have continued for years before realizing these once-blinded parts. The purpose of sacred union is the humble face-to-face realization of where you are still very much you. Only within the sanctity of sacred union will you feel adult enough to open and humbly receive. In any other form of relationship you will walk away and have nothing more to do with the process. Yet within sacred union the baptism of fire burns as the beloved continues to show you the falsities and masks you have been wearing. This is one of the greatest gifts of sacred union—seeing where you were once blind.

THE VOICE OF THE FIRST WOMAN

There are many voices at each different spiral of the womb. The fourth spiral is where the voice of your womb changes into a universal archetype or goddess, for example, Anubis, Hathor, Kali, Mary, the Crone, or the Goddess/Mother herself. This change in voice is as surprising as when you first access the voice of the womb, which you had previously mistaken to be the voice of your spirit guides, angels, or even God. The change in the voice of the womb can be dramatic, or even androgynous in nature: it does not need to be either male or female.

As you change and evolve, as the womb opens and shifts physically, emotionally, and spiritually, you access deeper and deeper layers of the Original, or First, Woman, from where all life births. This voice of the First Woman, the Womb of Creation, Galactic Center, or *sarvayoni,* lies within all women, attached umbilically to and through each individual womb. This voice of the first womb begins to be accessed through the living archetype of the Crone in the cavernous Womb of Gaia, that which gave birth to Gaia, which in turn births all women and all men.

This voice can be seen by many as Masters that people "channel." In most cases, these are simply higher vibratory aspects of your own being. These states of consciousness are realized by you when you are willing to own and be responsible for these states of consciousness. People say "I've been talking with my guides" if they are not ready to handle the glory of their being, if they cannot own the parts of themselves that are truly magnificent. Rather than own that part of themselves that has access to all of creation, "God" gets projected outward, and little responsibility is taken for what is being created and accessed by you.

I knew I was entering the fourth spiral when I began to experience a physical boundary during lovemaking. I seemed to come to the end of my uterus, and there was no more space inside. I had reached the depths. My yearning for a deeper connection told me there was more . . .

My womb was shifting, as the lovemaking became uncomfortable, nearly unbearable. Even as I was making love the fourth spiral began to filter into my consciousness. I was peering into two worlds—my beloved's face and a vast cavern that was beckoning me in. Voices from another realm were being sounded amid my groans of loving pleasure. I could see the Shakti firing up my spine, I could see the subtle anatomy of my beloved, I could see everything. I could almost see love.

I entered a great cavern, which on first sight was daunting. There was nowhere else to go. Should I go back into the normal world or forward into the unknown void?

I stayed at the entrance to the cave for a while and used my discernment. I sensed that the sheer creative intelligence that creates this world was in the cavern . . . waiting to be discovered. I knew there was a part of me inside, and I was filled with an innocent curiosity to meet that aspect. Even amid the innocence, there was a solemn sense of immense power; a generating bass line tone filled this space. Like a deep thunderclap, the power of creation was getting louder, and yet more silent, with every step that I took. The only way to describe it was a silent roar, or the Thunder of Silence.

At the end of the cave a crone appeared. She was old yet able-bodied, and she was squatting on the floor playing with bones as if it were a game for her amusement. She knew I was there. She spoke to me without looking up: "You have to continue with a gentle love that is willing to be, with all your experiences, in complete innocence. Let go of all old ways of being and relating. There is no use remembering what worked in the past as it has all been dissolved now."

She then turned around, and I saw my own face as I would appear in my eighties. She then produced a glowing Star of David and told me this was mine. She had been keeping it safe until this moment, until I found her. She did not say what it was for; she just inserted it into my womb.

This first time, opening the fourth spiral left me exhausted. I needed all my life force to enter this place. The amount of concentration needed to tune in to these subtle frequencies was immense. When entering the fourth spiral, you must conserve your life force, gently stay with your sensory awareness, and don't stray, or you will lose the thread.

The Crone told me to rest and recuperate after this work, that whenever I felt tired, to sleep and take nourishment. She said, "Do not fritter your life force on unimportant matters. All that you have is needed for this deep venture." (A. A.)

SURRENDERING INTO NOTHINGNESS

The way of the feminine is to be in the body. Mater and matter are one. Mater brings spirit into form. Matter *is* spirit in form. We are wired to embody anything in any moment; and in order for this to occur, we must become transparent. Feeling secure in who we think we are is not transparent. Resistance is not transparency. Resistance is nongratitude for what is being offered for your evolution. How fully do you give yourself? Are you willing to surrender even your individual soul into divine will? Even the soul is a bridge from ego to God.

Can I, in my humanity and in my humility, surrender into my not knowing, asking to be melted and shown the way? Holding on to any form of identity stops transformation from occurring. How long will we continue wanting to be accepted by this matrix? Where is there still a need to squeeze ourselves into a box? What part of you still wants to succeed in the illusion? Jesus said there is only space in this body for One. Ego? Soul? Spirit?

Embodied beings are those who allow themselves to become empty so that they can access All that Is. Only when we hold nothing back does love take control as our guiding force, so we are used by a force greater than ourselves. When the divine is the active force, there is no longer a hole that needs to be filled. When we want or need nothing from the world, our relationships can be based in truth.

The importance of the womb in all its facets gave rise to one of the Buddha's sayings: "Buddhatvam Yosityonisamasritam," or "Enlightenment is in the Womb." Buddha said that his Dharma would fade and die away with the introduction of women to his teachings. So why would he say that enlightenment lies in the yoni and womb of a woman?

The Dance of Life is the dance of male and female, the yin and yang. When both are in harmony, the fluidity, harmony, and balance of opposing forces, of polarities, creates life. For us this harmony can come by our entering and losing our identity in the yoni and womb, literally being absorbed, nurtured, dissolved, and re-created from this immersion. Our bodies are birthed from our human mother; our souls are birthed from the divine or universal mother. To return to this means we become reborn, we become innocent, as all our conditionings dissolve and we are remade and reborn through the cosmic womb of all creation.

If we look at the word *Buddh-atvam,* we understand that *buddh* means "the light of intelligence" or "super-consciousness," and *atvam* means that "this will come to you." *Yos-it-yoni* means "through equal union with yoni." Here, *yoni* has a dual meaning, for yoni indicates the millions of transformative lifetimes you have come through. *Samasritam* means "acceptance." Acceptance leads to allowance, and allowance leads to embrace. Embrace is the gateway to surrender, which is a key to the fourth spiral of the womb.

Samasritam also means being equal to those who are dependent upon you, dissolving the egoistic sense associated with power, control, and inequality. The opposite of control is surrender to love, and inequality dissolves and is neutralized by placing yourself equal to all beings. *Buddhatvam Yosityonisamasritam* then means "illumination comes to those who surrender to love and who are brave enough to be born not only from the human womb of the human mother, of the flesh, but also from the universal womb of the divine mother." One is then reborn in the Spirit; in other words, to be twice born, or *dwija,* is the return to innocence, and both births meet in the fourth spiral of the womb.

THE FULLNESS OF WOMAN

The fourth spiral is where the fullness of a woman arises in all ways. It is where a complete woman is birthed and created by giving birth to herself and to something crucially *other* than just herself. She gives birth to something far greater than herself for the greater good of all beings. This is when all aspects of what it means to be a woman coagulate into your form.

One way to do this is to give conscious birth to a physical baby and become a mother with all the biological, emotional, and spiritual changes that arise from this immersing into the innate feminine. These hormonal, psychosomatic, and consciousness shifts deepen the female body into its innate receptivity and womanhood. Many women say that you do not know what it is like to be a woman until you have had the experience of birth, which is when a new set of eyes open. (This experience can happen, however, not just through physical birth. Many women share that the birthing pains they experience in womb retreats are similar to that of actually giving physical birth, and some women even re-experience their menstrual cycles after they had stopped in their fifties!)

THE VALUE OF CONSCIOUS UNION

The deepest way to do this is to have a conscious conception, conscious pregnancy, and conscious birthing with the beloved, a man steeped in honor, love, and consciousness. With these roles comes the position of wife, mother, and beloved. This may not be politically correct for these times where gender roles are confused, and men and women are confused with them. Men are trying to be women and women are trying to compete with men, and both sexes are divorcing rapidly. By each sex being what it is fully, then harmony and equality can be obtained through the feminine quality of surrender and the masculine quality of protection.

These roles and ways of birthing are being reintroduced again to humanity as more and more conscious couples find each other. However, this is not the only way to access the fourth spiral, just a way that is becoming, and will become, more and more attractive to many. Indeed, it will become the predominant way of relating and having a family this century as people start to revive these timeless practices that have been squashed by modern-day society. And this, in one sense, is easier than the other ways to access the fourth spiral.

The other ways to access the fourth spiral take complete dedication from the woman to be totally committed to God and a very conscious man who knows the womb intimately and who loves purely with wisdom, surrender, and vulnerability in order to support, nurture, and help guide his woman, and himself, through the fourth spiral. This is rare at this moment on the planet, rarer than the ability of conscious couples undertaking conscious conception, conscious pregnancy, and conscious birthing, but this too will change in time.

Since a very early age I always felt that childbirth was not part of my destiny this time around. I was told by many people, who were able to "see" my Soul history, that in my last time my body was wrecked with childbirth, and within this lifetime I would extend my natural mothering energy to all beings on this earth, and that humanity would become my children. As I began to approach thirty-five, I began to check in again. I searched high and low, for clarification and verification on this decision.

This process lasted the best part of four years. I felt all this motherly love arise, and again my question was, "What am I supposed to do with this?" Finally, underneath the hormonal natural responses, was this deep love for God, and the sheer necessity to give everything, because until I felt that until I had given everything, I would not be fulfilled.

I knew a child wouldn't take care of this great ache to serve humanity. Unless you too have experienced this feeling within your soul, these words may not make any sense.

So, finally I chose to harness all of my creative birthing potential of conceiving and raising a child into a passionate life of bringing back the truth about sacred union and encouraging and supporting others. With this decision I live my whole life dedicated to the Divine, which has been missing from our religious and spiritual teachings for too long now. The reason for its elusive mystery is because of the sheer power that sacred union, also known as Divine Marriage, brings us. "Divine" hints at what is possible here. When two enter into Divine Marriage, a third being is automatically invited in to the bridal chamber; that third being is God, Truth, Source, whatever you wish to call it.

You simply approach lovemaking with the desire to experience God. From that experience, you begin to see one another as God. Quite honestly, these things cannot be spoken about. They can only ever be known. (A. A.)

CONNECTION AS PROTECTION

As Spirit grounds itself more within the body, it promotes a deeper dissipation of negative thoughtforms and emotions, which are taken into conscious awareness and released. The challenges that one feels become internalized, able to be seen for what they are, and healed. One deepens into trust and feels secure in one's own self. One rises above the electromagnetic radiation of the technospheric modern world that limits, disconnects, and stifles one from fully connecting into the womb.

A whole realm of energies and ways of relating drop away. We feel protected because we are connected. As we become more connected, we become more invisible to negative energies. When you become integrated, you can become seamless and invisible at will, and all negative energies from within and without glide off you, as you are centered in your core. Meditating to integrate is vital at this time. To deepen, slow down, stop doing, and enter *being* allows the brainwaves to shift and change.

> *I exist in the darkness . . . the emptiness of space . . . the blank slate calling to be drawn upon with all the colors of the universe, all the songs of every heart that is connected. I want to create beauty and share it universally. That is what I do. I sing the heart-song of each individual and then interweave the notes into a symphony of and for humanity that is broadcast to the far reaches of the universe. When one of my sisters awakens, I am immediately aware and tune in to her song, weaving it in to what already exists.*
>
> *It is my deepest wish to be ever present on the radar of your awareness so that I can hold and gestate your dreams. My greatest joy is to nurture life, be it the gestation of an actual child or the life of a dream, an idea, a vision . . . (A. T.)*

BIOLOGICAL CHANGES AND THE HEALING OF THE WOMB

In the fourth spiral of the womb, the womb accelerates into a deeper physical and biological shift. Awakening is a physical and neurobiological phenomenon, as brain, spine, chakras, and organs change their frequency and cellular geometries. The same occurs to a womb. New cells appear and old ones die and transform as new cell configurations and geometries arise; birthing pains, cramps, actual physical expansion of the womb, womb discharges, and other phenomena arise. Chemicals and hormones change their flow, brain patterns change, and your cells start to separate out from each other, revealing more and more space within, a space that allows more love to manifest and be felt.

I received a call from my doctor saying that they had the results from my last pap smear test. They informed me that I had severely precancerous cells at grade 4. They called these abnormal results discaryotic cells and said that the first step in treatment is called a calposcopy. Grade 5 is the highest state of malignancy and this means having an operation immediately! So grade 4 is taken very seriously, and action must be taken fast if the womb and cervix is to be saved.

My husband and I set out a course of deep and immediate healing. I received a complete overhaul over the next three weeks; I was on a mission to save my womb! I changed my diet to 100 percent organic raw foods, as well as drinking the most highly potent green vegetable juices I have ever tasted! My husband also put me on a detailed course of womb healing, which involved womb pulsing, light transmissions, and sexual healing of the seven gates.

I received three womb pulses from him, which were painful. He is a big man, and I am a petite woman, and his weight pulsing up and down over my womb caused a readjusting of my spine. I have a very curvaceous spine that really is not such a good thing. His weight and pulsing straightened my spine, but not without me screaming in pain, releasing deep memories of being trapped and "held" in a form of prison. This was the first step.

The second step was to receive three light transmissions specifically to heal the womb, which wiped me out completely. I did not feel any physical sensations, just an absolute blackout; I was gone! These transmissions were designed to clear the womb of any negative cellular activity and are available to anyone. My husband knew and affirmed to me almost every day that my womb would be healed completely and that the abnormal activity was a result of the deep openings and healings that my womb was experiencing so rapidly since we met and initiated this deep process on every level.

This was a 24/7 process that had my full attention, every other day I was receiving various light transmissions, sacred geometrical activations, and removal of old cells and energies from within my womb, cervix, lower spine, and ovaries. During this intense period I also had to balance all of this inner work with plenty of rest and long nourishing sleeps.

Throughout this three-week period I was experiencing such turbulent levels of anger, frustration, and resentment. I was furious and wanted to consume the world in my destruction. I felt so overlooked and disregarded. I wanted to smash, tear, and rip apart all that is unreal and all the hidden agendas within people and myself. In one of my diary entries I wrote that "I wanted to tear off people's heads and rip apart their egos. Why, in a place of such beauty, do I experience such ugliness?"

I was savage and felt that by feeling this way I had become a waste of a precious life. I was seeing hell in the midst of heaven. These turbulent emotions were commonplace for me for most of this time. Every time I dropped down into a pit of despair, the very next day I would experience a divine healing wave of gratitude, an unspeakable forgiveness and healing. It was a rapid roller coaster of intense healing.

But by these reactions was the womb healing. My womb had taken all these bodily emotions and mental states, transmuted them, and in the process the biology of my womb had become "abnormal." I would imagine that it had indeed!

After these three weeks of intensity, I found a hospital in France where the staff spoke good English and was admitted to receive a calposcopy. This was a relatively painless experience, but when the pain was felt, it was deep and emotional. I was torn apart that I had led myself to be in this position. Slices of my cervix were being dissected, with no anesthetic whatsoever. Being an extremely sensitive soul, I felt the emotions of being neglectful of my sexual relations, irresponsible and impulsive. In a word I felt sadness, deep and silent sorrow. Here I was, legs open with a stranger using a light and microscope to look inside my cervix, while he gently removed parts of me with a knife.

Every cut brought a wave of remorse and sadness. My husband sat beside me holding my hand as I sweated and cried. He had the grace to tell me to speak to my womb first and let "her" know what was going to happen, and why. God bless the doctor, he was a kind and sweet man, and incredibly gentle. He was so worried that he was hurting me, but no, he was not hurting me. I was, and had been.

I was assured that this would not impair my ability to conceive children, and should the worst happen, only parts of my cervix would be removed. I was in a lucky position as it had been caught early. Sadly, many women can leave it too late between smear tests, and if so, it could result in the cervix and womb being removed if cancerous cells have taken root. I wish this on no woman, as it is so much a part of whom we are if we remember it.

As soon as I left the hospital I cried deeply, as I finally felt all the forgiveness that so desperately needed to be released through me. I intuitively knew that this situation had been caused because of all the womb work I was doing as well as the healings that were taking place with my husband while making love.

The biopsy went off to the laboratory, and I was assured that in five to seven days time I would have the results. Eight days later, these results did not come. Two weeks later I called again and still no results were forthcoming. Finally, six weeks later (!) the doctor at the hospital told me that the reason why the results took so long was because my cells were tested again and again. Because I was already at grade 4, it was taken very seriously, and they were expecting to see something . . . yet they just couldn't understand why my results kept coming back negative. Grade 0! I was clear and free!

So I am a living testament to the power of the womb. All of this would not have been possible without my husband, his teachings, and of course, my most wonderful womb and the sheer power of love. By being willing to investigate, feel once again, and forgive myself and others, I was re-born with restored health and an empty past. And the same is possible for you, and all women. There is no need to have your womb taken out: it can be healed through natural means as women throughout the ages have done. (A. A.)

Physical Manifestations of Womb Healing

It has to be said that womb healing is a physical phenomenon. Many occurrences can take place that can even be detected and confirmed by the medical profession. It is a biological change as well as a consciousness shift. I noticed that some of these shifts included:

- bleeding constantly for two months, and/or irregular menstrual cycles
- a polyp, or growth, inside the yoni/womb
- precancerous cells at dangerous levels
- actual physical muscular sensation, painful at times, of the organ of my womb and pelvis stretching and expanding
- feeling of blocks/old numbness dissolving and actually being felt while making love, and the carving open of spaces within the yoni and womb physically, emotionally, and spiritually
- seeing and experiencing different aspects of my womanly self being found, discovered, excavated, and opened
- random points of sharp, electrical pain in the ovaries as opposed to the deep, dull ache of the womb
- lower back pain in the space behind the womb opening in deep, throbbing aches
- increased sensitivity to anyone approaching the womb and wanting something from me
- sadness at anyone apart from the beloved touching your most precious, open, and innocent space
- actual contractions from within

All of these can and will happen when the womb opens and ignites, when it becomes alive. It is also a mark of womb consciousness becoming integrated with the soul and bodymind.

Specific Womb Healings

The methods I used to heal my womb of cancerous cells can be found on www.christblueprint.com, under the "Healing" section. One of these is the Womb Lock Healing. Our chakra system has three main energy locks, known as *granthis* in Sanskrit. These three energy locks are found in every human being and are a key part of yoga and meditation practices. The first lock is in the Root Chakra, and it governs our grounding, money issues, survival, family issues, safety, and abundance. The second lock is in the Solar Plexus Chakra, holding our empowerment, giving us the ability to be selfless, vital, and radiant. The third lock in the Throat Chakra governs our ability to fully express ourselves and to surrender our fear and our sense of separation to Universal Spirit.

The fourth lock is in the womb, guarding our connection to the higher chakras and the healing of our womb and to the nurturing of the body with light. In the release of this lock, abortions, old relationships, debris, and unhealthy connections to the collective womb of all women, the womb of the mass consciousness of humanity, can be released as the womb opens more.

For the womb is where we give birth from, to ourselves. The womb is the light generator of the body and the creator of joy. When it is clear and activated, we connect with the full, unbounded expression of life, healing age-old wounds in both the male and female consciousness.

A specific womb healing to dissolve these cells can also help. Going to a Shakti Circuit or Womb Wisdom workshop, the locations of which may be found in the Resources section, will involve womb pulsing, which has to be done in a supervised and safe way by someone who knows how to do it in order to be truly effective and deeply healing. Switching to raw, organic juices and foods to heal and cleanse the body and womb is always a good thing to do, and much information is available on that in the world at large.

THE WOMB OF THE WORLD

The Womb of the World is a vast, black, fathomless, rich space in the depths of Gaia from where all life originates. The Codes of Creation are held here, as is the connection between the wombs of all women. In this space we are dissolved and merged absolutely into the primal womb: we return home. In its watery abyss, in its fathomless rich depths, all secret knowledge, all keys, all the aspects of our darkness and light are kept in pre-seed form; in the unmanifest potential, before it becomes form. Thus it is also here that these seeds can be connected to and dissolved.

The Womb of the World holds things in embryonic form before it becomes a form in Creation. It is a container, a deep, dark, moist, nurturing, and safe space for forms to germinate before growing and blooming into manifestation. Within the Womb of the World are held the energy patterns for this entire planet, humanity, and all species on it. All your patterns before you were born are held here, and all the deepest transformative actions for humanity as a whole are held here, and birthed from here, by those brave enough, and surrendered enough, to be able to enter here.

The Womb of the World is the field of infinite possibility potential, accessed by seers throughout history, none of whom were scared to enter here. For men it can be different, as it means their dissolution and ultimately their regeneration, as Christ showed in his crucifixion when he descended into this space to be resurrected: from the Divine Mother's Womb.

The Womb of the World holds the DNA patterns of all life-forms within itself, as the primal ezoic soup from where all life originates, similar to the dreamtime of the Aboriginals. It contains the seeds of all life here on Earth within it, and by extension it is a gateway to the cosmic womb, where the patterns of all life are found in an unmanifested state before they are made manifest in form.

To access it is one of the greatest alchemical secrets of all time, known to the Indian seers, Tibetan lamas, the priestesses of Isis, and to Christ Yeshua and the Three Marys around him. It is in this space we can be made anew by repeatedly immersing ourselves within it and dissolving all we are within its vast embrace.

> *As I entered a transmission meditation, I found myself on the crater of a live volcano. I looked down and saw my feet clawing the edge. The heat of the molten lava burned my face, and the smell of sulfur filled my nostrils. "I am within this fire; you have to leave behind all that you love to see me."*
>
> *"Do you wish to know me, more than you can imagine?"*
>
> *"Will you jump? Have you the faith to enter this fire?"*
>
> *I knew this ancestral voice; I had heard this sound before, as it was the oldest part of my soul.*
>
> *I stepped off the crater and fell through the flames. It burned. I smelled my burning skin, but I was laughing, as none of it hurt. I fell and fell and fell, until eventually I found myself descending into the cave where I first encountered the Crone. Sure enough she was there, in the same position as when I left her, squatting and preparing some kind of concoction with bones and fire.*
>
> *Through the candlelight, I could see other women sitting together looking straight at me, while the Crone had her back to me. Even though she was turned away I could feel the warm welcome as I entered. I recognized that the three women were the Three Marys—Mother Mary, Mary Magdalene, and Mary Salome. The beauty of seeing them all together took me by surprise, and I spontaneously fell into a deeper meditation with them. All of us women communed together for what seemed like years, until the Crone broke the silence, asking me, "What did you come here for?"*
>
> *I asked her for a deeper vision into the womb and to help me become even more still and silent, to live more fully through me, to stabilize my outer self, and to stay true and connected with this inner reality. I wished to see the truth of people so that I might be able to guide them toward their freedom. But I needed this gift of sight and an inner strength to be able to administer the guidance to others with power, wisdom, and love.*
>
> *I asked her to show me something, to take me into a deeper place*

within my womb. She looked toward the Three Marys, and they silently nodded. She stood up and asked me to follow her. We walked over to a hole in the floor of the cave. She began to climb down and into a tunnel. I followed on hands and knees, crawling into the darkness.

We eventually came to a huge opening. As I stood up, before me I saw what I could only describe as a city. From a far hillside I seemed to be gazing down onto a sprawling city of images, sounds, activity, movement. There was life in all its forms—human, animal, cosmic, mineral, elemental, angelic, and nature worlds—all swirling together.

The Crone walked me right up to this city, which was encased in a gossamer-thin veil or membrane. She told me that this is Creation, that this is all that is happening in the World in this moment, and that by touching this membrane I could create Creation, by simply willing or intending it to be.

She asked me, did I wish to create something? I nodded, because I was having health problems and I wished to be clear. I placed my hand carefully onto the veil and saw the outcome in an instant. The difference here is that you do not have to imagine and generate the images, senses, and interpretation of your desired outcome with faith to instantaneously see it. It is instant. Boom, the creation becomes the created.

She then asked me whether I wished to go into the city. I looked in at all the chaos and she felt my hesitancy. She advised me that this was my next destination, and as I was so close now, why not take that next step? I asked her how I would get back out. She promised that she would wait for me, and when I was done she would pull me out.

So I walked in through the veil and was pulled into this hive of activity. It was noisy, brash, colorful, and the information attacked my sensory system. I felt overwhelmed with stimuli, as what seemed like a million images per second were seen. I saw rapes in Africa, kids in New York, corporate boardrooms, banking systems in Tokyo, domestic fights in homes, deer running across meadows, foxes returning to their cubs, the Sahara Desert, thunderstorms, ants walking in a line, whales dining in the ocean, wedding vows, sunsets, hunger, love, death, and babies being born . . .

You name it, I saw it all, in all the different pockets of the world. At first I was moved by all that I saw. The Crone called out, "You have to look on with no judgment, let it move right through you, do not move." I moved through all these scenes, witnessing.

I called out again, "What do I do?" "Give everything," she advised back. "Open your heart and radiate your love into everything that you see. Swamp the entirety with your essence. Touch every form of life. You are able to do this."

So I fell backward and floated throughout this landscape, opening my heart and seeing a radiating field of consciousness saturating it all. After some time, the Crone called me back to the edge of the veil, as it was time to come out. She penetrated the veil with her arms and pulled me out. I fell onto the floor covered in a sticky mess and collapsed with exhaustion. (A. A.)

You have just been into the Womb of the World. All that happens on and in the planet is happening right here. Through your womb, you can access this; all women have this pathway. All of the intelligence that creates Gaia is here; every fiber, every atom, every thought, every action, word, and deed is seen here. It is the soup of Cosmic Creation. All that comes to Earth has to step in to this womb first. Every being, human and nonhuman, has to step into here first of all.

Amun Ahom Am

I Am the vastness . . . the pure potential. I lack nothing, need nothing.
I am the container crucible of all alchemy, the current and the transformation.
I am the fertile fields containing already the seeds awaiting only crystallized intention.
I am the potential of your ability to manifest anything.

I am the immortal vastness in which the divine dance occurs. I am sublime emptiness, the eternal cosmic space between your every breath. I am the Garden. I am both the fertile ground, and the seeds of life lying dormant. I invite you into this garden to partner with me, to become the clever gardener—to become wise—you must learn to trust the Seasons.

I am all phases of the alchemical process. I am the crucible.

I am the canvas from which the spark of Shakti emerges.

I am what you have called mystery, only called because of your attachment to five senses.

To enter me you must do so naked, leaving everything at the doorway. You must leave all your attachments: your roles, personalities, accomplishments, preferences, expectations, your so-called knowledge, your memories, your woundings, your dreams, oh yes, and your families.

You must know, in so doing, you humble yourself into the very vastness that you are and suddenly you are congruent with the emptiness that is/contains infinity and you are ushered in to the realm of the beloved, where suddenly all that you left behind is remarkably transformed into its highest essence.

To create with me you have to leave everything at the gateway. Leave behind, in humble desiring to experience something greater than what you have ever known. Enter me. I am Love. Love's only partner is devotion.

Yes. I am the one you call Mystery. Become transparent, and you will pass through the demons, the guardians of the gateway. Remember: demons are your reflection. They are that aspect of you who stands in the way. As you allow yourself to disappear, so do they! Your own conscious disappearance will usher you immediately in. This is your worthiness.

Only in your trusting, your innocence, in leaving all behind will you become humble enough to receive the immensity of the kingdom that awaits you. Forgetting yourself means letting go. This terrifies you because you have fashioned yourselves after the directives of your mind. The mind does not listen. The mind is a doer, and has tried to build your temples on false ground. That which is truly worthy of remembering cannot be grasped by the mind. Remembrance is a function of the heart.

Do not speak of or grant any of your life force into the breathing or allowing of any thoughtform or memory that you do not intend to continue manifesting and flourishing in your reality. (T. A.)

Access

The initiation into the Womb of the World happens in three stages. One is by activating and being initiated into the seven gates to the womb (for more on this see chapter 6, The Womb of All Attraction). In this process, you align the pulse of your own womb with the core pulse of the Gaian and Galactic Womb so that they entrain and synchronize. Your womb, the earth's womb, the cosmic womb, all begin to co-create together.

This is a process of performing sacred womb practices and healing the womb through light as well as unifying the shadow and soul as the one entity that it has always been. This, allied with repeatedly immersing into the womb of the world, takes you through your darkness and then into Black Light. Women such as Mother Mary, Mary Magdalene, and Marie Salome worked with the womb of the world in order to birth the divine idea or thoughtform of the crucifixion and resurrection onto earth. Without these women doing this, Christ Yeshua would not have completed his work on Earth.

The second stage is by initiation into a Womb of the World portal after having done this essential work on oneself. The third stage, in conjunction with the other two, is through sacred union with a beloved, accessed through surrender.

The Earth Connection

We deepen our connection to the womb through our connection to the earth itself. Grounding and connecting into Earth's fields allows us to become free of earthly obligations and duties, managing them without getting stuck or tied down. Here we open to a bigger love on behalf of the planet and humanity in a real and tangible way, regaining our soul connection and power.

Relationships, attachments to family, and completion of worldly obligations are cords that keep you stuck in Earth's fields, unable to access higher realms and frequencies, which can be helped by chakra cord cutting. Opening the foot chakras, visiting sacred sites, and clearing out entities accelerate this process to connect us to the inner earth and the core of the earth.

Another big reason why people get stuck in Earth's fields is that as people physically die, they can be scared of going to hell or of being judged by God, which prevents them from continuing their journey beyond the earth's fields; they can get stuck in the earth sphere as earthbound spirits. If you realize that God is friendly and is not going to stand in judgment over you, then this will not be a problem.

For most people, it takes about three days to realize they are dead. That is why people have to go through ceremonies and rituals to help them realize they are dead, to prepare them for their journey to meet God. But if on the other hand fear is put into the person they will hang around. Once these souls move away from the earth sphere the remaining family members or loved ones can actually feel the release and liberation; they will feel a lightness.

The Earth Heart

The heart of the earth is a living, palpable, breathing being. We enter the Earth Heart through the heart that is in tune with light, Nature, and our biology. The easiest place to access the Earth Heart is at sacred sites that are relatively untouched by man, in the heart of Nature. The best place *now* to access these energies lie over the Southern Hemisphere, specifically over New Zealand. These sites that hold an energy of pristine, magnetic intensity in the heart. This can be overwhelming, so pure and deeply resonant are the vibrations felt in the heart, powerfully purifying, opening, and releasing.

This space of harmony, of ease, effortless synchronicity, telepathic connection and deep biological relaxation is where the body becomes light and effortlessly fluid in an underlying, soft heart space of compassion. When we walk like this it is as if we are not walking at all—it is just light vibrating, moving the body forward; the body ceases to be separate from the light that you are. This "walking in bliss" is when all dualities are harmonized, which is when you fully resonate with the Earth Heart.

When we are like this, we can serve others better simply through resonance. We help each other to be ourselves, dancing together in a "Music of the Spheres" where each cell, each particle, "praises" the other into being the wholeness they already are. When each one is conscious of their wholeness, we are more complete.

Entering the Earth Heart is a step where we realize, feel, and experience love as our connection to Earth and all peoples. We realize we love all of life. This is the initiation—realizing Earth is the Center, the ground for our Awakening, and in giving to Her we give to all, and ourselves. This landscape is a deeply felt prayer and vibration. When we move through such a landscape, Nature itself sings to us in choirs of outstanding purity and beauty, resonating through every cell of our biological bodies. Joy of simple beingness and communion with Nature are its hallmarks, and those who truly give to the earth receive such an initiation.

We feel this privately in our own prayers for humanity, and in deeds that reflect this. Even if we feel we do not know how to contribute or give in this manner, we can; it is quite simple. Go to your nearest town and walk down the high street. Use whatever mantra or prayer you feel as you walk, sharing this light with all others, becoming receptive to the field of the town you are in, and giving what is required to fill the gaps for others. Even if you do not feel this working it will be felt and heard by those who are open to it, and by Mother Earth itself, who gratefully acknowledges our efforts at supporting her, just as she supports us every day of our lives.

Certain prayers and chants in sacred sites can activate this dimension within our experience. Yet it is important to remember that this is already here, all the time—we are just opening our eyes to perceive and experience it. However, it is harder in a concrete jungle to access this vibration, simply because the concrete, numbers of people, and EM pollution block it out more, preventing the free flow of subtler biological light vibrations that keep the five elements of earth, water, fire, air, and space in resonant harmony.

Nature here holds the key to our evolution in the dimension of biological transformation and resonance with the collected fields of Earth itself, from the Core to the Noospheric belts surrounding the earth. Without this resonance in this age we cannot fully embody.

The Circuit of Offering and Prayer

In offering and giving of ourselves, we enter the Universal Circuit, where everything is constantly coming into our heart and leaving, going back into Gaia and the Universe. We can tune in to this circuit of perpetual giving and receiving, or we can receive and no longer give out. This is particularly true of many sacred sites, where people come to receive but not to give, or give as an afterthought. If we do not offer and give out what is coming into us we get stuck and the heart closes. If we just take and take from Earth, our hearts get smaller and smaller. The healing happens when both are balanced.

This love creates new life, a new form of harmonic biology found in our very bodies and DNA. One of the most potent forces we create as humans is the loving orgasm; indeed the Mayans say human orgasms move the Galactic Center! Thus one of the most powerful ways to access the Earth Heart is through conscious sacred marriage.

9
Gateways to the Womb of the World

Sacred Sites Across the Globe

Sacred sites have a key part to play in the grounding of our human wombs to the Womb of the World, the Womb of Gaia, the creative hub and center of this world's creations. Throughout history, groups of women from India to England, France to Egypt, Ireland to Australia and the Americas, have utilized the Womb of the World to harmonize themselves, their partners, and their communities to the living intelligence, love, and power of Gaia, maintaining the connection between humans and their home.

Listening to our own womb, allied with the Womb of the World, ensures we stay in balance with the flow of life itself. The guidance we can receive from this alliance ensures our successful creative, harmonious flow in relating and further empowerment in our health, career, and deepening in our life's pathway, all designed to lead us into the interconnection, peace, love, wisdom, and divine justice that an empowered woman brings to Gaia, and all people she comes into contact with.

A fully empowered woman is one with her womb and the Womb of the World. In this union she brings harmony automatically wherever she goes and deepens others into their own unique nature, often without saying anything. For the womb is preverbal; it does not need expression in the same way a man needs expression; it is more of a resonance, a feeling, a primordial knowing that activates others through this feeling, an often long-neglected, half-forgotten feeling that we all have deep within us that has become so rusty through lack of use, conditioning, and over-reliance on ways of achieving, doing, and acting in a man's world.

The sacred sites of the womb are numerous; some are known and some are unknown. Most are as yet untapped and are just being reactivated again. Some of the more well-known womb sites are Vaishno Devi in the majestic Himalayas in India, the Temple of the Sun in Teotihuacan, Mexico, the Isis Pyramid on the Giza Plateau in Egypt, the Moray Mystery Circles of the Andes in Peru, the Church of Saint Sulpice in Paris, the Avebury Earth Temple in the rolling green crop circle fields of England, the pentagram of Rennes-le-Château in the mysterious region of the Cathars in southern France, and an Egyptian birthing site guarded by Anubis in Australia. There are others in Sri Lanka, South Africa, and New Zealand that are just being reactivated now in preparation for 2012.

VAISHNO DEVI, INDIA

The holy cave shrine of Vaishno Devi, situated in the lower Himalayas, is a sacred site of the Goddess. During a dark period on Earth many thousands of years ago, the Goddess in her three manifestations of Kali, Lakshmi, and Saraswati, Goddesses of Dissolution, Abundance, and Creativity, combined as the Triple Goddess, pooling their collective *tejas,* or spiritual strength. A stunningly bright light emanated from this union, and a beautiful young girl called Vaishnavi emerged.

From her childhood she displayed a hunger for knowledge that was like a vortex, and which no amount of teaching and learning could satiate. Subsequently Vaishnavi started looking into her inner self for knowledge and soon learned the art of meditation. As she deepened in her meditations, she started to attract the attention of many and various beings. In her prayers she asked to meet God and dedicated herself to this goal. Soon after this, Lord Rama became magnetized to her presence and fervent longing. As soon as she met him, she recognized him as no ordinary being, but the incarnation of God itself. She immediately asked him to merge her into Himself so that she could become One with the Supreme Creator.

However, Lord Rama knew that she and the world she lived in were not ready for the gift she was created to give. Instead, he promised that he would visit her again after the end of his exile, and if at that time she succeeded in recognizing him, he would fulfill her wish. True to his words, Rama visited her again after being victorious in battle, but this time he did so in the disguise of an old man. Unfortunately, Vaishnavi was unable to recognize him this time and was distraught.

Lord Rama consoled her that the appropriate time for the revelation of her Dharma had not come and that the time would come in Kaliyuga, or this present time period. Rama directed her to meditate and set up an ashram at the base of the Trikuta hills in India to elevate her level of spirituality.

As predicted by Lord Rama, her glory spread far and wide, and people began to flock to her ashram to seek her blessings. As time passed, tantric Master Gorakh Nath, one of India's main teachers on esoteric Tantra and an incarnation of Babaji, or Lord Shiva, had a vision of the meeting between Lord Rama and Vaishnavi and became curious to find out whether Vaishnavi had been able to attain a high level of spirituality.

He sent his most able disciple, Bhairon Nath, to find out. Bhairon Nath, on locating the ashram, started observing Vaishnavi secretly, and as he became enamored and infatuated by Vaishnavi's extraordinary beauty and the attractiveness of her womb, he began insisting, begging, and pestering Vaishnavi to marry him. Eventually, Bhairon Nath attempted to kidnap Vaishnavi, but she decided to flee into the mountains to continue her meditations undisturbed.

She entered a womblike cave, high in the majestic, serene Himalayas, and entered deep samadhi meditation for a cycle of nine full months. Meanwhile, Bhairon Nath, who was looking for her ferociously as only one who is infatuated and obsessed can, found her cave, yet met his ultimate fate when the Goddess, just outside the mouth of the cave, beheaded him. As he died, Bhairon Nath prayed to the deity to forgive him.

The Mother had mercy on Bhairon and gave him a boon that every devotee of the Goddess would have to have the blessing, or *darshan,* of Bhairon Nath after having the darshans of the Goddess; and only then would the pilgrimage of a devotee be complete.

After this, Vaishnavi decided to shed her human form and, assuming the face of a rock, immersed herself into meditation forever. Thus Vaishnavi, in the form of a five-and-a-half-foot-tall rock with three heads, known as the *Pindies,* constitute the Sanctum Sanctorum, or Womb of the Womb Cave, in modern-day Kashmir, India.

Vaishno Devi was certainly held in high esteem by the most powerful, loving, and wise sages of the day. Lord Rama, the Incarnation of Vishnu before Krishna, and Master Gorakh Nath, Incarnation of Shiva and the preeminent teacher on esoteric Tantra and probably Shakti Tantra and the occult in India at that time, certainly would not have shown interest in Vaishno Devi unless she had special power or potential. To have two avatars looking out for you is certainly a sign that she was the Goddess Incarnate. Both Rama and Gorakh Nath were waiting for her to mature, to ripen and blossom. This certainly had to do with the womb, which she was created for in Virgin Birth by the combined power of all Three Aspects of the Mother, as well as being what she was hunted for, and almost raped for.

Bhairon Nath was sent deliberately by Gorakh Nath to test Vaishno Devi and to be tested to see whether he was ready also to access the power of the womb. The power of the womb at the third spiral is all attractive, all pervasive, and can drive even the most balanced man crazy, as the opening of the womb means that both man and woman involved in the process have to be clear and open sexually, be balanced in their polarities, and have an open, unconditional, and pure heart connected to their sexuality.

Even today women who have this quality of an open womb are pestered to be married by strangers who have just met them and are harried by infatuated admirers displaying the classic Bhairon symptoms. As Vaishno Devi left the world to deepen her meditative training and immersion, she entered the womb, ready to give birth to herself, to conceive, in the cycle of 9 months, or 270 days. However, she was disturbed by Bhairon, the tantric disciple out of control with his passions, and was forced to kill him or be killed and raped. As he died, she forgave him, saying that anyone who wishes to know the Goddess and the power of the womb also has to experience the trials and tests of Bhairon in order to merge with her.

So in order to open the womb, the ultimate prize of Creation, one has to experience and pass through the trials of lust, infatuation, intense polarity, chaos, and obsession for the goal, the object—her. This portrays some essential tantric teachings—that we have to experience and move through all faces of life, good and bad, and learn from them all. Energy without goal, desire without an object for it to be projected upon or trapped by, is the free-flowing energy of life, of liberation, of the Mother Herself, continually creating for the sake of creating—in joy.

It was not time for Vaishno Devi to release her gift to the world; she was not ready, and maybe the world was not ready. The world, and Vaishno Devi, are ready now, because we are in the last phase of Kali Yuga, where she can finally merge with God in the guise of Kalki, the sum total of all the thirty-three million Hindu Gods and the last Avatar of God in this final cycle of history. The womb, and woman, as prophesized by Lord Rama, will be activated in this age on Earth in a way that has not happened for many thousands of years. The womb is now ready to birth what was seeded many thousands of years ago by the combined forces of the Divine Feminine.

This cave of Vaishno Devi is regularly visited today by millions of pilgrims from across the world. It is narrow and difficult to crawl through, covered with icy water throughout its length, representing a vagina and womb, or *yoni* and *garbha,* and is called Garabh Joon. *Garabh* or *garbha* means "womb or cave," where the creation is conceived, and *joon* is slang for yoni, the entrance and exit for the womb. It is said that if anyone crawls through Garabh Joon he can wash away all his past sins and is reborn, regenerated. For some, Ma Vaishno Devi is the womb from where the universe manifests.

AVEBURY, ENGLAND

The Avebury stone circle is one of the largest stone circles in the world and one of the most important ritual centers in Britain. It has been used for thousands of years as a place of birthing and as a sacred space for man and woman to sexually unite. Both man and woman are represented here by twin earth energy lines that create this sacred landscape temple. These twin energy lines are known as the Michael and Mary lines, crisscrossing England and meeting in a dark, wet, subterranean womb chamber in Avebury known as West Kennet Long Barrow. Just outside this barrow is where many crop circles are created.

One striking circle, created just fifty meters from the barrow on June 21, 2009, depicts the union of male and female, light and dark, in the yin yang symbol.

Inside the barrow chamber lies the main altar, built of wet, porous, resonant granite, where the Michael and Mary ley lines meet. Inside the chamber lie several antechambers, one of which was used by couples who used to travel from all over Britain to join in sacred sexual union. The other chambers were used for solo meditation and preparation for the rituals that used to happen here. At the spot where the Michael and Mary lines meet lies a huge portal, an opening into the mystery of the womb, where thousands of rituals are still being done to this day to enter these deep, dark depths.

Many birthing and sacred union rituals took place here, involving priestesses and the sacramental use of menstrual blood to link the moon cycle, the earth, and all the women participating together as one, through the use of sacred sound. The womb and both ovaries were reflected and used in ceremonial procession, where groups of priests and priestesses would walk along their ovary, chanting, holding flaming torches, and ceremonially laying their menstrual blood along the ley lines in order to consciously and vitally connect themselves to the Living Earth, vitalizing their own bodies with the landscape in communion and exchange.

This alignment kept both them and the earth in harmony and in full power. Even to this day, women who go there can harmonize their own womb cycle to the moon, regular as clockwork. Avebury was also used as a galactic clock, measuring the astronomical movements of sun and moon, which man and woman would then emulate, creating the macrocosm on Earth through the microcosm of the body, sexual energy, menstrual blood, and womb power.

Avebury is literally a womb inscribed into the landscape of the earth. The powerful earth forces all meet and merge here, to create an earth temple based on a vibratory sacred landscape. The energy of the womb and Sacral Chakra permeates the landscape, bringing up wounds of male and female, yet also providing a space for them to ecstatically unite. It is an enchanted landscape, both feminine and soft, yet extremely powerful once you tap in to it. The womb is formed by the main stone circle of the womb, and two ovaries, of which the feminine one has been partially destroyed, forgotten, and disused, its stones used as building material for the homes in the surrounding area.

The legends of Avebury go back deep into the mists of history, serving as a pilgrimage point for women and men who wished to enter the mystery of the primordial sexual and womb power. Clans of Owl Priestesses are known to have used this site in the past. Avebury connects to the heart of England through Glastonbury and the third eye through Stonehenge to create a triple temple of womb, heart, and mind.

Together these earth temples were used to lead people into full resonance with the living, breathing Earth Mother and Galactic Womb.

Today certain societies and individuals still use the barrow chamber for rituals, where people merge into the energy of the unified male-female energy through Earth alignment, sound, sexual union, and the use of sacramental psychedelics like mushrooms. When done on Full Moon nights, with the right intent, these rituals are potent and powerful as the womb in Avebury is connected to the Galactic Womb, with the barrow being actively used for thousands of years as an opening into the stars and stellar consciousness.

RENNES-LE-CHÂTEAU, FRANCE

Rennes-le-Château in the southwest of France is perhaps the most explicit womb imprinted on the landscape in human history. It is perhaps best known as the mystic setting where the Priory of Sion, a secret order that included some of the greatest names in science, philosophy, the occult, and art throughout history, gathered and made their principal domain. It is also the place that sparked the writing of *The Da Vinci Code.*

This whole region is shrouded in a veil of mystery, revered and inhabited by the Knights Templar and Gnostic Cathars, Christians who understood the unity of consciousness and held many occult keys toward this understanding. Yet even these ancient orders were preceded by greater beings who initially marked out the sacred sites here, which the Templar then used.

The womb at Rennes-le-Château has been fought over and speculated about ever since Saunière, a priest at Rennes-le-Château's small chapel, discovered hidden scrolls underneath the church and overnight became fabulously wealthy after speaking with high-ranking Christian dignitaries. Even at that time Rennes-le-Château and its surrounding area was populated with many sacred sites, ranging from the Devil's Chair (similar to the Devil's Chair in Avebury), the Tower of

Magdalene, Pech Cardou, and Mount Bugarach, seen as a cosmic portal and with many reported UFO sightings around it.

A few hours down the road are some of the most sacred feminine sites in France, at Les Saintes Maries de la Mer, where the core disciples of Christ fled to after his crucifixion. The disciples included Mary Magdalene and Mary Salome, as well as several other key disciples, all of whom built the world's first church here. The cave where Magdalene spent much time is also nearby.

All these beings were drawn to Rennes-le-Château for its womb, its creative power. The womb of Rennes-le-Château is marked out and inscribed in sacred geometry, specific sacred sites, and the art of numerology. Its key sacred geometry is the pentagram (which in Hebrew is represented by the number-letter HEH) for the womb, and the key numbers are 9 and 27—numbers associated with the cycle of birth. In the womb geometry found marked in places many miles apart all over Rennes-le-Château and the surrounding countryside, all aspects of the female sexual organs and womb are found, from the labia lips to the hymen, clitoris, cervix, vagina, and crescent womb itself.

All these geographical points, marked by churches, temples, mountains, and sacred sites, create a perfect womb dedicated to Isis, the Mother, symbolized by the numbers 8 and 18. This womb shape comprises a labyrinth with 15 nodes, a pentagram-hexagram of female and male united, and several crescent-shaped womb structures that create a perfect circle within which all else is contained.

Why is this womb particularly powerful and been held as such by some of the wisest men in history? Did they know the power of creation that the womb held, using it to their own purposes to gain power, wealth, and immortality? Certainly there were some lovers of women within this group of men, da Vinci being a notable example, and all of them recognized the power of *wombman,* a term we have remembered for woman. The original people who built the whole womb geometry must have been worshippers of the Goddess to go to such lengths to celebrate the feminine and her life-giving power.

In the story of the dragon guarding the treasure and the maiden we understand that the dragon was guarding a seed, which all wombs do, the seed of life. All points in the womb lead to the fertilizing of a seed, a seed that when activated and blooming has the power of Creation, the power of light, the power to create form and anything in the material world. In fact, the womb is the basis of the material world.

This geometric evidence, so precisely described in David Wood's remarkable book *Genesis,* directly confirms the womb story of Vaishno Devi, who can only be entered and fertilized when the lustful infatuated Bhairon, her nemesis, is included in the journey to fertilization. In other words one has to be whole, integrated in light and dark, to be beyond both and be the Light Bearer, able to open the Ark of the Covenant. This gift is only open to a man, a noble knight and king, who has true love, a love that runs through all polarities, light and dark, animal and divine, an unconditional love that includes the sexual and the spiritual.

For many the ark is said to be buried at Rennes-le-Château, and for others this ark is in fact the tomb of Christ, transported here after the Crucifixion. Is this why so many people have spent so much time in constructing this gigantic pentagram and all its associated geometries, castles, churches, and fortresses? In fact, some feel, as David Wood wrote in *Genesis,* that "the Ark of the Covenant is the womb, and it contains the gift of Intelligence," and that this is why the Knights Templar, the Guardians of Jerusalem and Knights of Christ, protected it.

It is important to note that the geometry at Rennes-le-Château is linearly imperfect—it has a very slight deviance. When the light and dark meet and fertilize each other, this slight gap is created in the web-like matrix of the world, a slight gap from where we can leave the womb, to come into the outside world, to be born.

When we truly unite the male and female then we enter a new creation, a new type of human being beyond being a slave to polarity and in unity consciousness. Here we can be both male and female whenever it suits us: hence the geometric irregularity, because in this state of consciousness we are multidimensional, fluid, and free, not bound by any law or rule of the third dimension, of rigid form. In the activated womb, we are free from constraint, free to enter a new world, whole.

The whole pentagram of Rennes-le-Château and its surrounding area is a gigantic womb, full of alchemical potential and transformation for those who are ready to venture within and use these arts. In doing so one can bring all of oneself into unconditioned love by raising and encountering all that is not love. Many relationships break down here as the basis of the relating is not love but need, healing, or attachment. Those relatings that are based on love can go even deeper with the alchemy of the womb, which is how, and why, this place was built—not for treasure or intellectual mysteries, but the greatest prize of all: human awakening and transformation into love.

THE CHURCH OF SAINT SULPICE, PARIS, FRANCE

Christ who is priest in the Virgin offers himself to God the Father through Her hands. . . . During all eternity, we shall be consumed in her while offering in her, and with her, the Son of God to the Father . . .

Mémoires pour servir à la vie de Monsieur Olier,
manuscript of Saint Sulpice, Rue du Regard

Saint Sulpice, Paris, is the beginning of the Roseline, or the Paris Meridian, the line of time that runs through some of the most important sacred sites in France, stretching to Mount Pech Cardou, the supposed tomb of Christ, and Poussin's tomb near Rennes-le-Château, the site of many of the Magdalene or Feminine Mysteries.

This church is built around a womb. The main feature and altar of the church is a huge womb within which stands Mother Mary and Christ Child. Within the confines of this huge womb, which literally measures twenty feet by twenty feet, are many little children, all ensconced and enfolded within the womb's warm embrace.

It is from this womb that the Line of Sanctity known as the Roseline, which marks the birthing of the major Magdalene and feminine sites in France, is born. The Roseline first came into major prominence through the activities of Sauniere in the 1800s, the priest of Rennes-le-Château who built the Tour Magdala and other sites dedicated to Magdalene and the feminine there. His masses were celebrated by famous personalities far and wide, because they included the feminine within them.

The Roseline comes to rest at Mount Pech Cardou, one of the five main sacred sites or arms of the Feminine Pentagram at Rennes-le-Château. Pech Cardou, or the Corps de Dieu, is supposed to house the body of Christ Yeshua within it, brought back from Palestine by the Knights Templar for safekeeping and to create a major energy vortex within Rennes-le-Château.

The Roseline marks out the major sacred sites in France, and this has been known for many centuries. The fact that it has become associated with the Paris Meridian of time, similar to the Greenwich Mean Time line, or GMT, is also significant as all time is measured from the womb, for birth inevitably means death, and the time we have to live is limited between these two constants of existence. The Roseline and its beginning mark out the space between two worlds, the difference between GMT and EU time. This difference of one hour also marks out the difference in thought structures between the island of Britain and the continent of Europe, which are significant for those who travel between both places and ways of being, attitude, lifestyle, and happiness.

The Roseline begins at Saint Sulpice. In this church stands the pillar that marks this line, and a huge womb from where this form of time is birthed and from where this timeline's creations arise. All of Creation's children birth from the womb, and the birthing of the Feminine Line in France arises from here.

Saint Sulpice is a heavenly, light-filled place, full of timeless peace. A sanctuary that sits within the busy cityscape of Paris, it illuminates softly and gently. Perhaps most well known from *The Da Vinci Code* book and film, Saint Sulpice is the site of many mysteries with its obvious clues of womb and time, which need the deeper understanding of Womb Wisdom to understand and decode.

Looking back at the history of Saint Sulpice, the emphasis of the French School of Spirituality, which was founded here through Jean-Jacques Olier (1608–1657), was on the nine months during which Christ lived in the womb of Mary. These men felt that the mystery, beauty, and depth of communion between Mary and Christ during this cycle was paramount to understanding God, Creation, and the nature of creating, as between Mary and Christ Her Son all things could be shared and laid to rest. This communion was understood to have been one of heart to heart. "The Incarnation is the first mystery of Christ; it is the most hidden, the most exalted and the least known. For this reason the saints called her womb the throne-room of God's mysteries. Consumed with the desire to give glory to God, his Father, and save the human race, he saw no better or shorter way to do so than by submitting completely to Mary."

According to other Saint Sulpice texts, "the pains and the sufferings which had been foretold by the prophets would affect herself, and that the same suffering that had to kill Jesus Christ would also kill the priest who presented him that day in the Temple, namely herself." In other words, Mary "felt herself too charged with their sins and obliged to make satisfaction for their sins." Mary here was seen as equal to Christ through the womb that birthed him, which was known as the "throne room of God's Mysteries."

Perhaps some of these mysteries are still to be found within Saint Sulpice, or perhaps they just point toward the most reliable place you can find it: within your own heart and womb.

THE CENTRAL COAST OF AUSTRALIA

One of the more remarkable and least known womb sites in the world is in the central coast of Australia, two hours north of Sydney. Situated in woodland, one walks through unassuming scrub until one reaches a rock outcropping. As one climbs up, one enters a narrow passageway carved out of granite, where Egyptian glyphs are carved on walls that span only a few feet across.

The many and varied glyphs end with a large and unmistakable portrait of Anubis, the Egyptian god of the underworld, Guardian of the Divine Feminine and Womb of the Isis Pyramid in Egypt, and guardian deity of secret knowledge. He is pointing to the sun, with its rays illuminating the landscape. As if to emphasize this, right next to Anubis is the symbol for the Neter—the Egyptian symbol for the gods.*

Anubis is one of the sixty-four Neter, or Creation Gods, also known as one of the sixty-four DNA codons that create the human DNA. He was revered as both the guardian of secret knowledge, knowledge of the Divine Feminine that led into the deep mysteries and powers of creation, and the guardian of the powers of death, both of which are connected to the womb.

As one walks through the narrow entrance to the site, one comes to an open plateau overlooking the sea, where, carved into the rock, is a womb chair large enough for a person to lie in a fetal position. Leading down from this birth chair is a fifteen-foot birth canal carved out of the rock, leading to a vaginal opening. After one has received their initiation while in the birthing chair, one then slides down the rock, through the birth canal, and then out through the rock vagina to be greeted, and celebrated, by the awaiting midwives waiting for each initiate to claim their right to rebirth themselves.

This is quite an experience. As with all womb sites, it is designed for rebirthing ceremonies through sound, breath, and light transmission through the priestess or priest, accompanied by all the women holding space and sounding specific sounds to accentuate the rebirthing process.

---

*The Aboriginals know nothing about this place as it predates their knowledge and expertise. To them, it is a mystery.

This womb site is talked about in local myth and legend as being connected to the Pleiades star system and was used many millennia ago to birth humans as we know it today, almost like an interface between Neanderthal man and present *Homo sapiens.* It is a powerful site that when used properly can lead to openings in consciousness and to the experience of being rebirthed.

TEOTIHUACAN, MEXICO

The Pyramid of the Sun in the magnificent and immense temple complex of Teotihuacan sits on top of the entrance to the Womb of the World. Ongoing excavations have revealed an alleyway running through the pyramid, with a central opening right underneath the summit of the pyramid. No one is allowed in there at the present time, but it can be accessed from the summit of the pyramid.

One would think that the entrance to the Womb of the World was at the nearby Temple of the Moon, or maybe even at the Temple of Quetzacoatl, supposedly the main temple in the complex. This assumption belies the fact that the masculine is the best guardian and protector of the feminine as seen in Anubis and the Knights of the Grail legends.

The Temple of the Sun (masculine) holds an energetic infinity loop between itself and the Temple of the Moon (feminine), where both polarities meet and exchange their polarities. These polarities are held within the huge energy field of the whole temple complex, which is accessed through the *ba,* or heart-soul, above the Crown Chakra. In this exchange of polarities, which can only be experienced and given access to by the Guardians of the Temple (not contrived or conjured up), which are serpentlike figures, lies the key to the mystery.

As one immerses oneself in this connection, one is allowed access to the Womb of the World at the summit of the Temple of the Sun. It is accessed through the womb/hara and certain geometric configurations that are created around the energy bodies that then allow the descent and access into the Sanctum Sanctorium of the womb. This process and key has been kept guarded for millennia by the Guardians of the Temple and can only be accessed by a pure heart and surrendered mind.

In accessing the Womb of the World, everything stops. All sound, thought, outside influences, sensations, feelings, and even time ceases. Everything stops as one drops into this space. To seed the womb, or to fertilize the seed already held in the womb, results in the release of that seed into the world again. This does not take many people, just one or two who are clear.

Teotihuacan is now open again for those of pure heart, surrendered mind, and noble intent, dedicated to giving. Giving is the essence of loving, and giving without wishing for anything back is how the Womb of the World responds to human beings. Those individuals and groups who wish to visit this place must become pure first, and then they will be given access. The gifts for the world, and those individuals, are simple: unconditioned, powerful, and pure love.

MORAY, PERU

Moray is about fifty kilometers northwest from the sacred valley of Cuzco, near the town of Urubamba, Peru. Moray itself is a massive and astonishing series of three different descending or spiraling circular structures constructed in deep wells of earth nestled among a range of large hills in the middle of nowhere.

Each of these craterlike series of concentric circles descends to a maximum depth of around one hundred and fifty meters, as deep as a fifty-story skyscraper. As one can see from the photos, some of the circular craters start from higher levels of the ground, while others start lower and go deeper. The largest depth within a single crater is thirty meters, roughly equal to the height of a ten-story building. (Interestingly, the temperatures differ as much as five degrees Celsius in the different craters on the different levels.) One has to actually descend down from ground level into earth itself to stand at the bottom of the crater, where ancient rituals of connection to Pachamama, or Gaia, took place.

The most impressive and well-tended of the three circular structures is not actually the most powerful portal to the feminine. One has to use one's inner eyes and ears to feel which of these is the actual portal.

Where, by whom, and how these circles were carved remain a mystery, yet they stand as an impressive testament to the wisdom of a sacred tradition said to derive from Atlantean times. Legend recounts that as Atlantis sank beneath the waves 13,000 years ago, a group of Atlantean Wisdom Keepers fled their ravaged continent, taking their wisdom to Egypt, South America, and Tibet, where monuments and artifacts of their existence remain to this day. Various legends abound naming Peru as a home of the Andean Masters, as well as preserving remnants of the ancient Lemurian continent, mystery schools, and way of life.

Peru is also next to Chile, where the Kundalini energy of Mother Earth has moved to in the past decade. The renaissance of the Divine Feminine and Womb Wisdom shows us that South America has a major part to play in both the ancient and new energies. When both come together, then a new world will be birthed. And this is happening right now, as the Womb of Moray strengthens its ancient connection to the "new" feminine energies and the diamond grid patterns of the Unified Field.

The womb well of Moray plays a part in this new birthing. It is a multidimensional portal to multiple levels of existence, and its orbs of light, diamond grid patterns, and even figures of light can be seen clearly. In the ancient creative ceremony with the womb here, undeniable manifestations of light occur, tearing open the veils to the many overtones of our multidimensional universe.

As you move through the rings of Moray, using them as navigating tools, you descend downward into Gaia, allowing the womb to be the guide to lead you through these pathways. Each circle acts as a force to be consciously aligned with so that you might be pulled deeper into the center of the circle, the center of Gaia, and the center of Self within you.

Once fully in the center, a form of co-creation can occur with Gaia, a co-creation that comes from the Divine Plan, which needs willing and surrendered human beings to act for the benefit of all beings. This is the importance *now* of Womb Wisdom and womb sites: the next step in our evolution occurs from our conscious co-creation with Earth itself, and the feminine capacity of birthing. Men can only seed: women do the birthing, and when both come together, a new Earth and a new civilization will be born. The foundation for this birthing is what we walk upon: Gaia. And it is from our union with Gaia in our hearts and wombs that new birth occurs.

The heart is not enough. The mind is not enough. The womb is not enough. Being eco-friendly or Gaia-friendly is not enough. All four principles have to come together through the fifth, that of birthing/dying/resurrecting, in order for the pentagram of alchemy and creation to manifest clearly. Approaching it just from the heart, hoping that all will be well, is a renunciation of one's own responsibility and conscious awareness; approaching it from the mind and womb only, without the willingness to surrender, to die, to create anew, only sows more confusion, leading to theories that cannot be tested, proved, or put into direct action.

The human womb, the Gaian womb, and the Galactic womb are the missing links in our evolutionary cycle, overlooked and forgotten by a mentally dominant society intent on an abstracted, a politically and spiritually correct, lifestyle. Yet they were once the focus of many sacred traditions and helped to keep their societies in harmony with Gaia, their own core wisdom, and the larger cycles beyond Gaia.

Moray was built to harness these many-dimensional levels of creation and focus them into one space, place, and time, through groups of people and the earth's womb itself. Harnessing these many levels into focus takes a holographic awareness. And the ability to work consciously on up to twenty-three levels simultaneously helps one to open and sustain a viable matrix.

This matrix, *matrix* being another name for "womb," is a Diamond

Matrix. The Diamond Matrix is the pattern for the Unified Field, a field that is supported and bloomed into existence and manifestation through the Womb of Gaia and the unified focus of human beings. When enough people are focused and unified on this objective in womb sites such as Moray and are using the innate technology of the human system and lightbodies (see *The Nine Eyes of Light by Prakasha,* for more details) then an ancient, yet timeless template is activated, which can be seen as new to our present-day consciousness.

This technology of the womb and lightbodies is not something you can just stumble upon or hope to channel or do once you are in such sites. It is a treasure that has been held in ancient sacred lineages, forgotten even to most of the modern-day holders of many of these lineages, which have become more patriarchal and mental in their way of working with the more superficial layers of the womb and creative capacities that are lying dormant in most people.

Moray is an ancient treasure of connection, creation, and manifestation that has been lying inactive for many centuries and which has now been activated again. The ways to access it are held in the womb of women and the hearts of men, and the union of the two, which is why it has been inactive for so long. The key to the birthing of an enlightened future lies in these mysteries of the past, and the magnificence of the human heart allied with the wisdom of the womb is the bridge between them both.

ISIS PYRAMID, GIZA PLATEAU, EGYPT

One of the most powerful portals for the Womb of the World and the Galactic Womb is the Isis Pyramid on the Giza Plateau in Egypt. This is because a whole pyramid has been constructed on it, as in Teotihuacan, to amplify and harness its energy. Directly in front of it lies the Sphinx of Anubis or Anpu, Guardian of the Isis Pyramid, son of Osiris and adopted child of Isis, her most loyal protector, and the Guardian of the Duat/underworld and of secret knowledge.

The three initiations into the Galactic Ba, or soul, of Osiris are the most well-known initiations today and are received in the Great Pyramid. In the Well, the initiate would confront their deepest fears, to then travel into the Queen's Chamber where one would harmonize and integrate this journey. From here, one would enter the King's Chamber where one would receive initiation into the Divine Masculine Christ Consciousness, or Ba, through alignment to fourteen different star systems, all mapped out through the star shafts built into the pyramid.

This would then prepare the initiate to work with the Womb of the World and the Ba (soul) of Isis in her adjoining pyramid. Only by having completed the previous three initiations was one prepared enough to enter the Womb of the World and the power of creation, manifestation, and dissolution held there. This pyramid has not been active for thousands of years, as most have forgotten its purpose, and how to work with it in the patriarchal age.

The Isis Pyramid is connected to the Moray circles and works in a similar way, albeit deeper and with a more specific purpose. The Isis Pyramid is used potently for initiation into the Womb of the World and the seeding and connecting of this womb in alignment with the conduit of a human womb to the star systems of Andromeda, Arcturus, and Sirius. When this happens it is felt and seen.

The Isis Pyramid in the Giza Plateau is one of five gateways to the Womb of the World. Situated between the Great Pyramid and the smallest pyramid, it is very much an unknown, veiled, and mysterious entity that few people ever go into to do sacred work. It is directly guarded by the Sphinx of Anubis, the most loyal adopted son of Isis. If you look clearly on the Giza Plateau, you will see that this Sphinx of Anubis is actually directly in front of the Isis Pyramid, *not* the Great Pyramid. Why is this? Could it be because the Isis Pyramid holds the greatest secrets and treasures? Why has it been so covered for so long?

Robert Temple in his recent book, *The Sphinx Mystery,* reveals much of the wisdom behind this in detail and how the Sphinx was actually Anubis. The question still remains, however: Why is Anubis guarding

Isis, and by extension his father, Osiris? What is he guarding?

The Royal or Divine Feminine, as the Grail Mysteries attest to, needs a loyal protector and guardian to help shield her purity. Only the purest, most noble and loving humans are allowed into the inner sanctum. To all others, it is a mystery that cannot be seen even if it is right in front of their noses. The Womb of the World is a most precious sacred sanctum, holy and divine, and needs protection from the curious and those intent on using it for their own power fueled agendas.

This is why it was closed down thousands of years ago, to prevent it from falling into the wrong hands and being used to create less loving scenarios for the world. Power is power, and once power is accessed only the pure of heart can share and transmit the Will of the Divine, that which is concerned with the procreation of life, love, and connection between all beings. Those not pure of heart will try to use it for their own agendas and to garner power for themselves.

The Isis Pyramid, constructed to lead to the Ba (soul) of Isis is a downward-pointing triangle, whereas the Great Pyramid of the Ba (soul) of Osiris is an upward-facing triangle. The Isis Pyramid is a chamber for seeding, incubating, and grounding energies into the Womb of the World that then aligns to stellar energies through the conduit and medium of a human womb, while the Great Pyramid is for celestial communication and transmitting outward.

Inside there is a sarcophagus, which is where a gateway to the Womb of the World awaits those willing, prepared, and trained to take this initiation. This chamber is one of the most powerful places on Earth where the Black Light resides. Black Light is the purest and richest form of Divine Love. It is a form of love that cannot be spoken about, simply only ever experienced. We have both experienced this Black Light as a final resting place, the Divine Ocean where one can truly let go as we dissolve into it. With all lights extinguished, you can fall back and into the Black Light, which seems to permeate every cell, as well as the spaces in between. You simply cease to exist as you become one with the rich, all-enveloping darkness of love.

In this state, all self-identification comes to an end, the mind rests in nothingness, the body drops and deeply relaxes as the Soul guides you gently through the deepening layers. The breath is amplified within the sarcophagus as the walls create a sound chamber all around you. This deep breath can be used as a guide to take you deeper and deeper into the earth, down into the great depths of Gaia herself.

Within the sarcophagus, when spiraling into the Womb of the World, you may begin to hear many other sounds and voices. I experienced sounds of the deep ocean, the prayers and sacred mantras of all the women before me who had entered this space and initiation, the breathing and soundings of whales, huge quantities of water above and around me, and the sense of being drawn deeper and guided onward.

I used my womb as my navigation tool, longing to connect my womb to the womb of the world, yearning to find my true resting place within the great womb.

Lying in the sarcophagus is a timeless experience. When I was graced to have the experience I felt that I never wanted to leave. I felt so complete, fulfilled, and dissolved; it took all of my strength and commitment to come back into being, get up, and leave.

Silent tears were flowing into the darkness as I realized I was pure, untainted consciousness, resting, flowing, and docking into the great Womb of the World. When you find your way to the Womb of the World, it is as if you are given back to your true Mother. The love is unspeakable, the embrace cleanses all lifetimes as the Mother soothes away all hurts and pains of this world.

I experienced a physical connection within my womb as I docked into the Womb of the World. My breath changed, it became fueled by Shakti and passion as I began to experience a deep sense of being touched by the great Mother in my womb. I would not say the experience was sexual, as no desire was involved, but at a certain point of feeling the Shakti pouring through my physical body, I began to sense a deep womb orgasm beginning to arise.

This sensation seemed to bubble up from the Womb of the World, up and through my womb and physical body. When I experienced the orgasm it was one of pure celebration and gratitude. In my experience I was laughing and crying silently, huge laughter and endless tears of joy.

I now know that something changed forever within me at that time, a permanent change as that experience now lives with me every day. A way was carved open, and my soul and womb now know the way home. This can only happen because my womb became the conduit between the stars and the earth, and I had my beloved with me. Love is the key.

The Black Light, or the Black Love, is a quality of energy that dissolves, embraces, and transmutes negativity back into its purest innocence. It is important to know that it doesn't change "bad" into "good," as within the Black Light all duality ceases to be. Black Light simply strips away all harm, pain, and disharmony and transmutes it into a clear, impeccable innocence.

Black Light is also a carrier wave for incubation, seeding, regeneration, and resurrection. You can place things within the Black Light to rest, germinate, conceive, and eventually give birth to. It is the highest love to rest in and to literally die into, in order to be reborn.

For some, the Black Light may conjure up fears of the unknown, fear of the dark, fear of "evil' or dark forces, as in the West we have been conditioned to believe that darkness is dangerous. So this boundary will have to be crossed to get to the true essence of what the Black Light holds for us. The best way to cross this terrain is to connect deeply to your soul and human heart and breathe steadily as you overcome these fears and hurts. These fears are mind based, so do yourself a great service: by soothing and nurturing your mind you can assist it through the layers of conditioning, easing out the tension and pain.

A deep pool of dissolution is awaiting you all. There is a place just for you, waiting and breathing . . .

In the past groups of people's sufferings would be felt, accepted, brought within the womb and transmuted through the embrace of the wombs of a group of priestesses working here. This too is how collective transmutation can occur *if* enough women can activate and heal their wombs and bring them into union. The pyramid was also used in conjunction with groups of male priests in order to facilitate journeying into the Black Light and the Womb of the World, for many reasons.

When one is initiated into the Womb of the World in the Isis Pyramid, one enters Black Light. Black Light is the light of the universal womb, before light visible, before color, before matter as you know it. Before there was light, and an idea of darkness, lies Black Light, the sweet silence of the beloved calling you home.

It is sweet emptiness, the heart surrendered. It feels like your heart is gently but perpetually breaking wide open, with no object for its breaking. It is crystal clarity, pure, deeply touching, and feminine in vastness. There is no object for its love and compassion, for there is nothing there, no reference point, no concept or form, nothing to hold on to, no memory, no past, no future.

It is the deepest intimacy one can ever know. It embraces you, not you it. It touches you in places nothing else can, and nobody else ever will. It makes you cry, for it is the deepest remembrance of love a human can ever have. It is the beloved that has no face, no form, and no substance. It contains itself completely within itself, pure before it becomes form.

It is only by means of your passage through matter that you evolve. While you are in the stage of your evolution subject to the push and pull of the body-mind, or matter, the womb to you is the Mother of Sorrows, because all your sorrows and troubles come to you through your contact with matter. But as soon as you lose your identification with the bodymind, then the Divine Mother manifests, uncloaked as Black Light.

Within the womb lies the power of the sun god Ra, and within the centers of all suns themselves lies the seed of the Black Light. Suns are grown from the Black Light, and when they explode into supernovas they return into Black Light. The Black Light is the beginning and end of Creation. When you are born, you come from Black Light in your mother's womb. When you die, you go through the Black Light as the soul makes its journey back to the Creator. It is Isis herself that shares knowledge of this beautiful alchemy of the Black Light.

The Black Light: A Message from Isis

The Black Light is the light of the universal womb, before light visible, before color, before matter as you know it. This Black Light is my body; it is what I am clothed in.

I Am everywhere. Everything is made of me. Everything comes from, is bathed in, and made of me. What am I? Love. The universe is pervaded by love, it is love, and everything within it is an expression of love. This Love I Am is tender, loving presence, holding you, gently unfolding all that you are, containing all that you are in my womb, the Womb of the Universe.

Before there was light, I Am. Before there was an idea of darkness, I Am. The Black Light, the womb of the universe, is where all births lie as a seed jewel reflected in each woman's womb. This seed jewel of empty vast fullness, of pregnant potential, is the ocean that holds all within it. This Black Light is where I come from and is who you are.

Black Light is the sweet silence of the beloved calling you home. It is sweet emptiness, the empty heart surrendered. It feels like your heart is gently but perpetually breaking wide open, with no object for its breaking. It is crystal clarity, pure, deeply touching, and feminine in vastness. There is no object for its love and compassion, for there is nothing there, no reference point, no concept or form, nothing to hold on to, no memory, no past, no future.

It is the deepest intimacy one can ever know. It embraces you, not you it. It touches you in places nothing else can and nobody else ever will. It makes you cry, for it is the deepest remembrance of love a human can ever have. It is the beloved that has no face, no form, and no substance. It is the magic of nothing within the loving field of everything. It contains itself completely within itself, pure divine thought before it becomes form.

It is only by means of your passage through matter that you evolve.

While you are in the lower stage of your evolution, subject to the push and pull of the bodymind, or matter, I Am to you the Mother of Sorrows, because all your sorrows and troubles come to you through your contact with matter. But as soon as you lose your identification with the bodymind, then I Am for you The Divine Mother, as I Am now uncloaked.

This subspace of the universe lies within your own cells. The 94 percent of dark matter lies within your own self. To access it requires courage and dedication to venture into the unknown through the portal of deep silence and stillness. It is a diving into the depths, unafraid to lose yourself in the blackness that envelops you, and dissolves you into the nothingness. Without this passion to be consumed by the eternal vastness, it is not possible. In this age, this passion will be seen and noticed, and extraordinary help will be given to those that are genuine in these ways.

Within the womb lies the power of the sun Ra. What you do not know is that within the centers of all suns themselves lays the seed of the Black Light. Suns are grown from the Black Light, and when they explode into supernovas they return into Black Light. The Black Light is the beginning and end of Creation. When you are born, you come from Black Light in your mother's womb. When you die, you go through the Black Light as the soul makes its journey back to the Creator.

The Black Light is the power to create from the space where all things are held in potential before they manifest. Black Light is the greatest alchemy and the most powerful magic of love, the potential that all women hold within the womb. It transforms by holding and bringing everything that you are back into its pure, undifferentiated, unformed state—original innocence. In this state, all wounds can dissolve, and all things are made possible. All things are made new.

Connecting the Womb to Earth

An ancient practice done for many thousands of years is connecting the womb to the earth consciously. This is simple but highly effective and can be done at any time when you have twenty minutes free.

1. Go to a spot in nature that you feel comfortable with and drawn to—a sacred site perhaps, but one that is green and alive.
2. Lie on the ground, with your womb pressing against the earth softly but firmly.
3. Place your arms above your head and press your third eye against the ground.
4. Start to breathe out from the third eye, projecting a beam of white light with each exhale down into the earth.
5. Travel with this beam of light and the breath through the earth, through the soil, through the tectonic plates, down into the molten core of the earth.
6. Do this for five minutes.
7. Now breathe in through your belly, up into your womb.
8. Breathe in the green of earth into your womb, the lushness, the protection, the nurturance of earth. Allow yourself to feel comforted, rooted, and grounded.
9. Do this for five minutes.
10. Now, thank Gaia for helping you to be alive; thank her for giving you the ground to walk on and be nourished by. Thank her for giving you a body to experience life.
11. Ask her to support you with whatever is most important in your life right now; whatever issue or obstacle, ask her for her help.

PART FIVE

Infinite Spaciousness

10
Pure Freedom and Continuous Expansion

The Next Octave of Evolution

The Womb Speaks

I Am Nurturer, the One who Nourishes all.
I am Fertile, the sacred ground in which the Creator entrusts the seeds of life to unite, germinate and grow.
I am Cycle, and the Circle of Life.
I have no beginning. I have no end.
I am Vast Space, the infinite spaciousness of Divine Consciousness.
I am Sacred Waters, the ever-flowing Waters of the Ocean of Creation.
I am Chosen, the Gifted One, designated to Receive and to Cradle the Inspirations of the Heavenly Cosmic Mind.

I am home. Your first house.
It is my wish that You remember
You can return to me always
for rest and comfort, peace, protection.

> *I am Invitation, the invitation to the great Earthly Dance of ecstatic love.*
> *I am Power beyond Measure. Of Source, not Force.*

The First Movement of Creation is pure joy. Joy that has no reason or cause to be joyful—just by its very nature it is. This subtlest and most powerful creative wave as it manifests into the dynamism of living form is the pulse constantly humming behind all life, the throb and tremor that give rise to all waves of life.

This fluid, causeless joy erupts with no reason. It is bliss, bliss that has no reason to be blissful—it just *is* blissful. Dynamic, orgasmic, rich in infinite potential and feminine, it is the primordial wisdom in all life. When we live in this stream, we live according to our heart's desires, our innermost urging and true calling, following our inner voice and listening to our natural rhythms as they weave and connect back into their source.

Living within the fifth spiral is felt as pure freedom and continuous expansion. All boundaries and limitations do not operate here. A freedom that constantly reveals and unveils is experienced within and without. Duality ceases to be; all is met with the same pure innocence, an untainted curiosity, with the power of discernment and authenticity.

The human life that we have known is taken to the next octave of evolution. Living in the fifth spiral is a gateway to humanity's ascension.

Life slows down in the fifth spiral, and the drags and pulls of the 3-D world have no hold here. Nature opens and reveals herself as the cosmos literally pours into you. Beings deep within the earth and the cosmos become known to you, as you are now vibrating at a frequency where true communication and communion unfolds. True seeing becomes your new sight, inner listening your true dialogue, and the love of life radiates out of every cell. You are simply alive with a love that is unhindered and whole. Ribbons of light flow from your being, as you connect with life on Earth and beyond. You are here to give.

The simplicity of this experience is spellbinding. There is nothing to get, but all to give. This giving fills your entire being, building like an orgasmic wave, filled with gratitude for your human life. This experience could never come from books, lectures, or following a guru/teacher. This bountiful place is awaiting your radical actions, your witnessed commitment to reach this place. By declaring that you relinquish control over your life, abandoning the parts that are holding you back from this place, only then by standing for the truth and freedom of your soul shall the fifth spiral unveil herself right in the middle of your life.

From a fragment of his writings that still remains, we learn from the ancient Greek philosopher and poet Empedocles that "the Nature of God is a circle, center everywhere, circumference nowhere."

THE INTERCONNECTION OF ALL OF LIFE

The womb is a perfect circle. The circle or sphere is the shape of all matter and energy, visible or invisible. In the circle all life interconnects in a continuous, unbroken stream of fluid consciousness. Here any identity, anything, can be at any other point. This means we can be anything at any time, as all points in the circle can be at any other point within the circle, and the circle is everywhere. Yet it is nothing.

If we draw lines radiating out from a perfect sphere, they meet in an optical illusion known as *pragnanz*—a circle that is there but not there as it is not actually drawn but formed by the lines themselves. The lines are the vacuum, or void, in movement, the initial directions of light that happened after the initial creation of our universe.

These are described in quantum physics as null lines, the paths taken by light rays and massless particles. A geometry based on null lines is the Grail of quantum physics, for in a universe having such a geometry, mass does not exist. All null lines always have zero length; scale and distance are also zero. In other words, all distances, times, and ideas of large or small, micro and macro, no longer exist, and therefore no time would elapse from traveling from one point to another.

In these terms not even one second passes from the time you leave, say Sirius, to Earth, for along such a null line the distance to the stars is zero. When you look along a null line, nothing separates you from all that you see in the Universe around you. In fact you are everything that you perceive around you in all directions—there is no separation.

As the visionary scientist Buckminster Fuller said, "All vibration, all the spheres of material things, are like radio waves expanding on a fixed wavelength into the fluid weightlessness of space."* Here both modern science and the world's sacred traditions agree: the Universe is but countless spheres within spheres within spheres, the "bubbles" of material creation, as the Buddha said.

Each of these spheres is created as like when a pebble is dropped into a still pond—each ripple, each undulation, each concentric circle created is a different vibration, a different frequency, a different world. It could be said that each one is a different sound, holding a different meaning. We are at the center of all of these ripples, looking out at the waves and effects our thoughts, feelings, and actions have in all directions.

At the center of the sphere, our core, the life spark within all of us, pushes toward movement. These movements constantly go through us and the earth and are made conscious when our emotional state is agile and we can easily emote, for emotion equals energy in motion.

For us to align to this wave requires that we become fluid. When we are fully fluid, we can experience any feeling whatsoever at any time, at will. Thus if we can, at will, produce equanimity, delight, love, anger, or tears without charge or attachment to them, then we can be moved from within by the Spirit that is always fluid and open. However, the less we can summon feelings, the more we are frightened of them, the

---

*A good introduction to the ideas of Buckminster Fuller's is his *Operating Manual for Spaceship Earth,* written with Jaime Snyder.

more we are at their mercy; conversely, the more we allow ourselves to experience feelings, the less we can be enslaved by them. If we allow them to pass through us, we become transparent, without charge, without holding on to anything or anybody.

Thus we learn to move the body, feelings, and mind so that Spirit can move us. In this fluid individuality we can be any aspect of consciousness, or anybody, at any time, for we are able to feel and express whatever we are needed to be in any given moment, to express all parts of our universal character; in effect we become "all things to all men."

THE BLACK HOLE

At the center of our Milky Way galaxy lies a massive black hole. The size of our galaxy, and many others, is inextricably intertwined with the size of the black hole; the bigger the hole, the bigger the galaxy. Scientists and cosmologists are now saying that black holes birthed our galaxy and possibly even our universe.

All light, waves of time, all energy gets sucked into a black hole's infinitely dense point of concentrated mass, becoming a singularity, a total one-pointed focus. All matter becomes pure energy, and everything unifies. In our perception this is known as the Bindu point, where all aspects of consciousness, all parts of the fragmented mind, all parts of body and soul, converge into a one-pointed focus. The actual experience of this is the experience of being created moment to moment, changing all the time, like being reborn in every moment. This then leads to deep stillness, peace, and bliss.

Time slows down near a black hole. If you and some friends were in a spaceship orbiting a black hole, and your friends ventured into the black hole while you remained behind, you would notice that their movements and wristwatches would become slower and slower as they approached the black hole, until, right at the event horizon, they appeared frozen in time, or totally still.

This black hole has been prophesized to be in direct alignment with

Earth within the next decade, which will initiate a new phase of evolution for humanity. Once sucked into it, it is said that we are able to see the history of the whole Universe flash before our eyes, yet once inside, one would be unable to communicate anything of this to anyone not in this state. Perhaps this is why many great mystics have been unable to communicate to ordinary people, choosing instead song, koan, or paradox to explain their experience of the inexpressible.

In the cosmic womb lies unified matter, or "true matter," the substance that unifies matter and spirit. As John said of this age in Revelations, "It is the time of the substanceless coming into substance, and substance to become substanceless," where form becomes emptiness and emptiness becomes form, Perfect Wisdom.

This universal womb manifests form from the formless through the medium of the seed. In entering this space, we are annihilated, and we can then resurrect. This is the greatest pain that one can feel, but it leads to the greatest freedom. Emptiness is the gateway to the Black Light. Emptiness is the heart of all things, the Perfect Wisdom. All forms are temporary. Everything neither arises nor dissolves. Form does not differ from emptiness, and emptiness does not differ from form. Form is love, and love is empty.

All things are empty; never born, never ceasing, neither pure nor impure. There are no forms, no feelings, no thoughts, no perceptions, no consciousness. There is nothing to see, no ignorance, no ending of ignorance, no cause of suffering, no end of suffering, no path, no witnessing, nothing to own, and nothing to attain. From here all is possible, yet nothing needs to be done.

CREATING THROUGH THE BLACK LIGHT

When any of you create anything of great impact or huge significance that truly taps in to universal forces and power, then you have to enter the Black Light to birth this. If you do not enter the Black Light, then the creation you are birthing does not have full influence; it may be useful for some people, it may even have awareness among the masses in your Earth, but it will not change anything fundamental in consciousness. This is a marker and a test for you to remember.

The Black Light, as epitomized in the form of the Black Madonna, is the state from where all realities come from. Christ, Buddha, and other Great Ones have all had to enter this Black Light to bring forth their transformative actions onto the earth plane, to ground these actions onto the earth plane.

For the quality of the Black Light is the power to birth realities and create through magic, wonder, and grace. Every birth, the first and most momentous journey, begins in darkness. Just because humanity has forgotten about it for the last cycle does not mean that it is not here. It is the height of all alchemy, the heart of transfiguration.

When both partners in a sacred relationship immerse themselves into this velvety fullness that is empty of experience as you know experience to be, then Sacred Marriage occurs. It is in this state of being that you both recognize each other as God fully, in every cell, in every fiber, nook, and cranny of your body, mind, and soul. It is here that you remember and join with those Ones, like Yeshua and Mary, who have merged together in the Black Light before and are still there in that space waiting for you to taste what they are living.

Other ways to immerse completely in the Black Light are taught to Egyptian and Tibetan initiates. In Egypt these initiations were given to those who had completed the first part of the Black Light in the Pyramid Initiations and were ready for the next step. In Tibet these initiations, through mantras to various Dakinis (female tantric deities) and female Buddhas, such as Ekajati, are given to those Bodhisattvas who have conquered the fear of death.

INCUBATION/GERMINATION

Germination is the slow and tender growth of creation after a period of dormancy. In the West people are programmed to want everything fast and immediate, yet Creation herself knows the true pace of life. There are places within you that are lying dormant, tender, and vulnerable that need careful tending to in order to develop into strong and powerful attributes. By taking these young seeds of your being and placing, or rather nesting them deep into the Black Light of being, you can leave them there to germinate and incubate over time.

We all know the gifts of our soul, whispers of your mission and message while here on Earth, the inner visions of what could come to pass, the innate and unique qualities that have been given to you: take these inner knowings and place them within the Black Light.

When you have developed a strong connection to the Black Light you will be able to look in and see each seed's development and growth. It will become second nature, something that is with you at all times.

Like a true mother, you can sense your creations and make changes once your seed has come more fully into existence. When you sense the time is right, the moment for birthing is ready. This is a very sacred moment; give yourself time and solitude to harness the true experience that is about to come. Use your womb and cervix to push the seed out from the Black Light in the womb, and literally birth this aspect of your being into creation.

As with a true birth, a sadness or grief may be experienced, as leaving the black light can often be painful. It is, however, a glorious pain, a pain soaked in gratitude and awe.

Rest and fall into the experience, take the whole day off, disconnect from the world and gift yourself this chance to witness and wholeheartedly experience it.

This incubation/germination aspect of the black light can also be used for "holding" your beloved's seeds and aspirations. He can place his seeds deep within you, by intending that his "seed" is moved into his semen. He can ejaculate into you when making love, and you can then take the seed deep into your womb for nesting. Ask your beloved to describe his seed, what it looks like, its color and shape, so that you too can keep a watchful eye over it. Before agreeing to do this, make sure you know fully what his seed is and feel for your inner response, whether you feel it's appropriate or not.

All this work has to be in accordance with the highest laws of Light and Evolution, a giving to the whole, not for the individual, as it represents a part of the divine plan for you, for him, and for the whole of creation. Selfish agendas and needs will cause a split within you, a split from love into shadow.

If you are not physically able to make love, his seed can also be given remotely through transmission or meditation if you are physically apart, or by placing his hand on your womb and intending it to drop into your belly. Again by watching and "nesting" over the seed, you will know when the time is right for birthing, making sure every step of the way you are keeping your partner informed.

When you are birthing, create a sacred place for you both, with no distractions. Open to the Black Light and include him in its field. Cover the two of you in Black Light, stemming from your womb. Take your time, there is no rush. Spend time together in the Black Light, bathing and resting in its embrace. Feel the closeness between you, close the gaps, experience no veils between your two forms. Together you shall birth this seed. You both need to lie on your backs, genitals to genitals, with the woman's legs over the man's legs.

Make sure you hold hands to keep the heart connections unified as one heart. Push the seed from your womb, into the lingam of your beloved, and then he must take the seed up and into his hara. This is a Divine moment.

RESURGENCE AND RESURRECTION

Within the Black Light you will find the keys of regeneration and resurrection. The deep, penetrative, and soaking Black Light has the power to reawaken huge quantities of vitality and replenishment deep with the physical and lightbodies. The richness of this fertile and potent energy has the power to create a full reemergence within you, your beloved, and, over time with guidance and clarity, with many others.

To enter this gorgeous space, simply enter in to your womb, preferably in a darkened room, and sink deeper and deeper into the velvet folds of pure pre-creativity. From the core of the womb you will find a womb beat, a pulse or throb of the pure woman, her essential self, what it means to be feminine, what it means to carry the feminine seed of creativity.

Use this pulse to engorge yourself with Black Light, saturate your cells, fill the spaces between the cells, submerge your whole body, your soul, your mind, and your past, present, and future all into this deep, dark light.

Rest here, barely breathing, dropping the body, loosening the mind, and discovering the soul ever deeper. Take the Black Light into the center of every cell, see yourself being restored at a subatomic level, layers upon layers of your being, surging with pre-verbal life.

When extending this space to your beloved, the same steps are taken, the only difference being you are extending the Black Light to include his entire range of bodies. See the two of you in your enlarged womb, like two fetuses before birth, before formation at the conception stage. Weave the Black Light into your beloved's structure and dimensions of consciousness. It is important that your beloved is lying in your arms, or with his head on your womb. Encourage him to curl up like a child or surrender into you as the representation of the Divine Feminine. Feel yourself as a Cosmic Woman, huge with an eternal depth. Create a field around you of an eternal love, like the rings of Saturn, slowly rotating and gathering. It is your role to encircle your beloved, to create a space of safely, protection, and of being held at a galactic level.

It is this Black Light that holds the planets in their position, which slowly spins the celestial bodies perfectly on their axis. It is precisely that which you are now offering to your beloved.

Only a woman can do this, only the womb can open to these enormous zones of resurrection and resurgence. By extending this to another, the woman opens to her true nature and design. Deep inside, all women know this. This role is woman at her most natural, her mind empty, her heart eternal, and the womb field endlessly extending.

For the man to truly receive, he must surrender to the woman. He must become like a child again when lying in the womb space. The woman must feel comfortable with this, to allow her man to lay down his strength, his sense of protection, and his idea of himself as being there for her. In the womb space, the woman is there for the man.

Take your time; there is no need to rush. Let go and let God soar through you both.

DARKNESS

A simple way for you to begin to open to the possibility of the Black Light is to spend more time in darkness. Sit in a darkened room in silence, or spend a day and night alone in darkness. Become used to its presence as a living, palpable force. In this darkness make it a practice to embrace the parts of you that arise in fear, restlessness, or judgment. Allow the heart to open and feel in a new way. Make the Black Light your friend. This is an extremely powerful and fast way to delve in to the portals to the Black Light and get to know yourself.

Making the Black Light your friend is going back to the beginning of Creation. In the beginning there was only darkness everywhere; darkness, the living waters, and the flow of these living waters when the Creator moved his light across them. This beginning of creation still lies in all of you today, existing in your bodies in darkness and flow.

The Black Light is the creative darkness from which all life emerges. We die into darkness, and within the darkness die into light, so birth and resurrection, regeneration, can happen. In accessing this darkness, and working within its silence, we guide life from emptiness into form.

In the darkness there is so much love that nothing gets in the way of it, nothing reflects it, or refracts it. It is pure, because nothing is there to block it, not even you; not even you are there to limit it. Within darkness there is no duality, nothing to reflect God's light. Therefore this light is there to birth into the world, into form, so that God may know itself, and that you may know yourself.

You can wake up in the darkness through many practices; but the most potent aspect is that in the darkness you become open, revealed, and vulnerable, becoming receptive to the inner pulses of life, of creation, and in doing so you merge into the nothingness, the darkness where we are not, yet which is our home.

A portal into the Black Light is known today by your scientists as the "adaptive unconscious," an interface between the 5 percent of your brain that acts mainly from habit and the other 95 percent that is a vast pool of unconscious power lying within you. This "unconscious" is mythological and metaphorical in nature, responding to interior images and symbols rather than rational thought.

In this flow thought dissolves into flowing movement, a fluid understanding and presence accessed anytime, and applied into any situation. Like water, fluid thinking envelops objects from all sides, subtly, sensitively, and gracefully feeling and undulating through all nuances of meaning and every detail of a form.

Many people today are enamored with light and forget about the darkness, the space from where all light comes, and indeed the place where you are born and nurtured during the first nine months of your life; in the womb. What you give form to in daylight is only 1 percent of what is seen in darkness. If you can access both of these realities, if you can enter into the process with courage and embrace all the visions and fears that arise, then you can be reborn.

John the Beloved demonstrated his union with Black Light through his surrender to the Holy Spirit, for to enter the Black Light is to be in total surrender. As John felt and intuited the time of his upcoming death, he ordered his disciples to dig a deep hole on top of a hill overlooking the harbor at Patmos, the idyllic Greek island he was marooned on. Mystified, they did so, and John asked them to accompany him as he lowered himself into the hole, whereupon he informed them that this was his last night on Earth, and they were to watch over him until the morning!

Astonished by his request they stayed up late into the night, listening to their teacher's last words to them. However, one by one they fell asleep in the early hours of the morning, to wake up at daybreak astonished. John's body was gone, snatched from the embrace of the earth itself! All that was left was an empty, black hole . . .

HEALING

For many of you darkness brings up images of the unknown, what you fear, what you have not yet embraced, what you sweep under the carpet and try to forget about. These locked doors of the human psyche that you fear to step in to actually hold the greatest potential for healing, growth, empowerment, and confidence, for when you fully enter and embrace the darkness, boundaries and limitations expand, dissolving anxieties and fears. Darkness holds a great deal of power, and empowerment, for you.

This complete immersion into the deepest darkness, that of the womb of the earth and the embrace of matter itself, is perhaps one of the most powerful means to instantly access a portal into the Black Light and in the process heal birth traumas, sexual abuse, and deep wounds. All of this is healed through visionary experience, visitation, and richly mythological occurrences while buried in earth's embrace *without* need for modern-day methods.

Children hearken back to this by burying each other in the sand. Doing this, burying all of you, is the first step toward submerging fully into the darkness and entering a much more expanded, healing, magical, and numinous world where you can speak to spirits past and present, communicate with your ancestors, and enter in to multiple realities simultaneously.

When many of you are in darkness together, you all become closer.

Many things are revealed about you in the silence, emptiness, and darkness of the Black Light, especially when others are present. All your conditionings and modes of behavior can melt and dissolve in darkness, which is when a whole new world of deeper relationship, peace, and wordless feelings communicate your hidden nature.

Sexual impulses and differentiation can become androgynous and unified as you reconcile your differences back into the night of creation. Here it could be said that light divides and darkness unites. When whole groups connect and communicate in this way, a family develops. As Christ said, "When more than two are gathered in my name, so there shall I be." If more than two gather in dark silence with the same intention and commune with each other, a deeper understanding forms.

Black Light creates a space that everyone can melt into. The woman holding the Black Light creates space, which the man then activates, ignites, and electrifies, bringing forth what is passively held into dynamic manifestation. This is how Yeshua and Mother Mary worked together, and later how Mary Magdalene and Yeshua worked together, in a different way but in the same principle.

The womb holds the space for you to expand into the infinite, into the Black Light, if you soften yourself enough, and allow your boundaries to become fluid, to expand out, and into, the embrace of space. Expanding in this space is like lying on a rolling, undulating bed of softly tolling bells, drifting in these shimmering vibrations, allowing yourself to follow these vibrations into the heart of the cells, allowing yourself to dissolve into the soft, empty space in the heart of each cell.

In this deep rest, Black Light brings Spirit into matter. This gentle but all-powerful light penetrates into and transforms matter, even under the most impossible of situations. Black Light holds, in the heart of the subconscious, a charge, a charge so deeply rooted in the primal brain that one could spend many lifetimes struggling with it. This charge is a denial of love that was required to bring spirit into matter. To truly bring spirit into matter requires that we go into the depth of this subconscious, this charge, and unfold it from within itself. One goes into illusion and penetrates it, allowing the full flowering of the subconscious into consciousness.

THE BLACK SUN

The Black Sun is the direct experience of the Primordial Feminine Force, the Womb of the Universe, and the Creative Pulse of the One. This Creative Pulse of Oneness is made up of three things: Love, Desire, and Self-Delight. Its mirror side, what we have to face and integrate before we embody, are anger, power and disempowerment, darkness, and extremities of all kinds.

In the Black Sun we face our deepest challenge: to claim our power directly from Source. This is the magical power of transformation. Here we have the uniting of all possible qualities, infinite potentials, with that which has no qualities at all, in the moment of birth and rebirth happening in each and every moment of existence.

Darkness holds power, and from darkness, light is born. Without power, light collapses, and love has no way of becoming manifest. For to become selfless, to have no self, requires that we are strong first—for selflessness is the greatest power of all, the ability to go into and experience all light and all dark, all faces of the One Self. Here we cannot seek, we can only welcome the experience of our false notions and judgments being ripped apart as we enter the Many and the One, the Feminine Matrix of Creation, "for by woman we are created, and it is by woman that we will be saved."

In this process we become a unique, self-contained aspect of God, an individualized aspect of oneness working in a manifested human form. When the male is fully centered in his infinite pillar, then these energies can dance around this pillar like a vortex. It is by loving another that one can truly love oneself, and yet it is also in loving oneself that one can truly love another; this is the dance.

The Womb of the Universe

Based on the 108 Names of Kali

My Mother,
Immeasurable,
Auspicious doorway,
Clothed in space,
Dressed in emptiness
Adorned only by vastness
The naked moment,
Birthing in every second renewed and continual

You create our worlds for pleasure, play, and our learning
You measure all worlds, you measure us into existence
You birth all worlds, you birth us
You nurse all worlds, you nurse us
You grow all worlds, you grow us
You dissolve all worlds, you are the end of us as we know ourselves
You mature all worlds, you are our maturing

You are our supporter, mother of the universe
Cause of bliss,
Golden
Destroyer of misery and poverty,
Bestower of eloquence, the power of speech
The virtuous bestower of magnificent desires
The rider of time, the dissolver of time, the creator of time

Slayer, mother, and nurse
Servant and sovereign
Authority and student
Worshipped and the worshipper

You live in the act in between
The play, player, played, and the playing
The magic of nothing within the loving field of everything

The power of Woman
Supreme and subservient
Dancing life into being
Serving and being served

The power that is unstoppable
Drunk on bliss
Wielding the cleaver that separates false from true
Untouched, unattached, by passion, yet the heart of passion itself
The red flow, death of the ego
Creator of fear, laughing loudly at its play
The luminous beauty of the eyes that see so clearly
Rolling with love piercing with gratitude
Flashing
Yet demure, deep, and enticing
In the softness of the lotus heart
Adorned with rubies glowing

Your form is the night of time
Eternal night, eternal rest
A bed where all identities come to dissipate

You are the authentic sound of Being
Creation resounding resonating
rumbling through awareness
The hum in the back of our thoughts
The hum in the background of our feelings
The hum as our bodies unite

Dominant in bed
Tiger footed in movement
Sure and agile
Graceful and serene
Hair wild and free flowing in all directions
You ride creation into being

As the power of time
You devour us, your children
As the power of time
You stand astride, resplendent upon the corpse of this universe
When we are born you are there
When we die you are there also
Eternally the same in the intensity of being

All our acts, all our fruits, come back to you Mother
Everything returns back to you
It is only our arrogance that stops us seeing truth as it is

All that is limited fears that beyond its limits
You as the creator of time, stand beyond time, beyond limits
One who is beyond all fear can protect us all from fear
As long as we identify with anything there is fear
This is why you are clothed in space
The dissolving of all fear into freedom

11
Birthing Out from the Womb

The Beginning of Nothing

The womb is a living metaphor for your transformation. The womb holds all within it until it is ready to be brought into form, into manifestation, into light. You are within one of the spirals right now, until you are ready to move out from it and be born. To birth yourself means you have to die, and this is the most radical act you will ever do in any lifetime.

There are two births, two wombs: the birth from the physical womb of your human mother, and the birth from the true womb of the universal mother. One is to be born of the flesh, one is to be born of the Spirit. Most humans are still in the journey of the second womb. To reenter it consciously is to move through its birthing journey until we arise out from it as an adult, not as a child still playing with its toys, mimicking the behavior of others to get by in the matrix.

Most people alive are still in this womb: unborn, unconscious, firmly trapped in their beliefs of what is and what is not. They are born into physical adulthood without even exiting the womb. Imagine this: a fully grown man and woman, say a friend of yours, still living in the womb, still a child, still not seeing or acting as an adult.

THE EGO DIES IN THE WOMB

Grasping, needs, holes, and attachments, also known as spiritual beliefs, keep you trapped like a hamster running around its wheel, searching for the next trend, the next teacher, the next thing that will make life a little better. And the wheel goes nowhere, except round and round. All you are doing is making the surface appearance of existence a little more palatable in the matrix, but the matrix is still there. It is like painting a few pictures onto a prison wall, placing a few meditation cushions on the floor, lighting some incense, hoping it gets better, hoping you are doing the spiritual thing, reaching some kind of peace of mind.

The only true peace of mind is not having one, and that involves death to the ego.

Being spiritually correct, being nice to everyone, leading the spiritual life, doing the prescribed things, you listen to the respected figures that everyone likes, read their books, go to their workshops, as they challenge nothing and tell you everything will be okay and that all is love and light. And you buy their products, as it keeps you safe in the vain hope that this is reality, a reality agreed to by you all, so it is true, right, and safe. Hope is the first and last thing to leave on the spiritual path.

But the prison wall is still there, veiled by the seething beast of your repressed shadow that is lurking underneath, carefully cloaked, rationalized, spiritualized, and hidden away deep within you. To touch it is to break the carefully constructed spell you and the world have agreed to weave around you . . . and when this happens, which it inevitably and undeniably will, there will be an almighty flare-up, judgment, anger, projection, and breakdown. And the whole spiritual thing gets thrown out of the window. Finally!

Returning to the womb means you die and get reborn. No lineage can bring you to this; only you can. To do this takes actions, not just words, philosophies, or intentions. Clearly state your intention and desire, and it will eventually come. You manifest it by surrendering to it, and when it does it will be destructive. In truth, as one starts the death-rebirth process of true and total transformation, it is destructive, destroying the old you to lead you through the womb, into birthing you.

This is not pretty as all parts of your life enter great upheaval. There is no salve, no need to put a Band-Aid on a broken arm or gaping wound as you enter this phase, no need to make life pretty, clean, and nice. No New Age prattle, no marketing spin, can take you through this, but anyone who is transformed has been through this and will catalyze this for others, as this is the greatest love.

To die is to live. To destroy the ego is to live in eternal life. For the ego to be destroyed is to enter true life. To welcome this, to ask for it, to beg for it is the beginning of the authentic spiritual path. Anything else is pretending to be spiritual and is fear dressed up in spiritual clothes. The quick fix leads to the longer term malaise. And yes, you have been wasting time if you have not been doing this, and there is no time to waste as time is your only resource and death is your only constant. And all of this is happening right now.

You have to die to all you are in order to be present here now. There is no good or bad, just what is, and you have to move with that. Returning consciously to the womb to die is a radical step. Within it you will find the deepest fears that most spiritual ways cannot address, as they are looking for a utopia, a happy ending to the fairy tale. The fairy tale is the ego, and the happy ending is when it dies. To cover up the ego with niceties keeps you in the womb state; to destroy these niceties is to leave the womb and become reborn.

Eventually you have to leave the womb and be born. You cannot do this as an infant but rather as an adult. What is an adult? One who has seen through the matrix of their own beliefs and has happily died to them, having dissolved their previous life to enter a new, unknown, yet free existence. This is radical, and it lives in action. It means you dispense with all that you have known and believed and even go beyond any kind of spirituality. You become a natural being.

The point of the womb is to enter it, die, heal, and become reborn, then leave it as an awakened adult. Most people are still living in the womb—they just do not know it; most people still have not been born, even though they have a plethora of teachings, techniques, well-being methods, and ways of "giving" and feeling good about themselves to prove it.

To be reborn means you get wiped out—deleted, erased, all previous traces washed away. Old life and person are gone. You become clear and clean. And people will not like you for this and will try to stop you, pull you back into their comfort zone. Either move forward or stay stuck. I share with people, "Stop going to workshops! Stop being a spiritual junkie! You can get this here and now if you give your all." And guess what: they still continue on the merry go round . . . you know why? Because to transform will mean the end of the "spiritual ride," and that is the last thing the spiritual junkie mind wants. It needs the hamster wheel to keep turning so it can feel useful, as though it is doing something worthy, noble, good, loving, and nice . . . all because it needs that "love" to fill its hole.

Love does not fill holes: it exposes them.

Yearning is like this too. It is an almost sadomasochistic urge from the hole within you to look/pray for something outside, pleading, even begging for it. It keeps reality and the deepest love away by making it something else to aspire toward, and, of course, the aspiration keeps the hamster wheel turning by keeping you in this apparently noble quest. And this has its place, up to a point, when it becomes self-limiting, limiting you from being and keeping you in doing and looking outside for what is already yours.

And what happens when this too dissolves? The breakdown leads to the breakthrough, a letting go, a deleting. Shock horror—there are no more teachings, nothing left to do, no more processing, platitudes, and breakthroughs, no more healing, journeying, or exclamations. What will you do? You are alone.

All the spirals show you the way out—by going in. Loss becomes the way forward, as everything gets stripped from you, and you die more and more to your cherished beliefs every day. It all has to go, and the degree to which you hold on is the degree to which you are denying truth. Truth hurts, but only the ego.

When it all goes, what are you left with? Nothing. This is when you are born, when there is nothing left to do. You are surrendered, and whatever wishes to flow through you does, even without your knowing it, as the *you* has been subsumed, forgotten, dismantled, and dissolved. This is the greatest service.

The womb holds a key for those brave enough to go the whole way and to be born. Birth means death, and these are both actions. How can you die today? Ask yourself this deeply. What is the very first response you get? Do it.

Get rid of it all. Start with the books, the clothes, the spiritual paraphernalia, the statues, the altars, the idols, the paintings, the residues of you on the physical plane. Do the physical body cleanses and fasts, eat raw, drink live juices, cleanse the internal body. Then get rid of the music, the memories attached to that, the photos, and the furniture connected to the past.

Now, after doing the womb mandala, it is time to die to old relationships that no longer serve you. Say good-bye to friends that no longer are where you are or where you are going. Cut the cords to old lovers, and maybe even present ones and marriages. Be ruthless and unerring in your aim and single-pointed focus. Do the Arc Line meditations and womb clearings on anything that no longer serves your growth. Kill your parents (metaphorically) so you can be who you are, so you can be born fully, and be who you are meant to be, which certainly is not your parents.

Now comes the time to let go of all the beliefs, the deeply ingrained baggage and engrams that create the structure of the mind, the foundation of the mind, that you haul around with you, the mental chains and voices that distract and sway you into judgment and fear, the shadow that sees on the outside what you do not wish to see within.

THE REBIRTH OF THE INNOCENT

Finally, divest yourself from the spiritual lineages you are attached to. Kill Buddha, kill Christ, kill the Goddess, kill Krishna. They just pointed the way to something beyond them, and that is who you are. To attach to the signs along the way means that you will never reach the destination, which is right here. Signs point the way, and the way truly is signless.

You no longer know or understand anything. All you know is that you are, and even this means nothing, or registers as anything. Everything melts away, blends into insignificance, and then into nothing. It was never there. There is nothing more to understand, nothing more to do. You become nothing, humbled and at ease with whatever is. "I Am" and "I don't know much of anything else" are the mantras, and it is true, as you are allowing everything to be what it is and for life to unfold as it does.

Whatever you had, or thought you had, dissolves. You may seem far away, but you are right here. You are totally normal to other's eyes, but seen by those who have been washed away as well.

"Wash my body, wash my mind, wash my soul," as the Lord's Prayer shares. When you wash something, all the colors, all the dyes, all the pigments fade away, leaving only the pure white garment, your original dress, behind. When you wash your body, you wash away anything that stands in the way of it and light. When your mind is washed, you leave behind your beliefs, resistance, needs for anything, your judgments, your fears, and your need to be somebody, anybody. When your soul is washed, you give it up to God, not knowing what may or may not happen, but trusting, surrendering, and letting go.

This is innocence.

Die to the ego, die to yourself, to be reborn innocent. This is the message of Womb Wisdom, and it is this that makes a timeless woman.

A NEW LIGHT ARISING

The light at the core of creation, the light of the world or the Womb of the World, is coming alive to create a new way of being and working, a new hologram of creative light, life, love, and power that surpasses all the previous ways that we have known throughout this cycle of history. This is a new awakening light within life itself, a new light of life, where the life flow itself teaches us and becomes seen as an extension of God/Source.

We can influence these new patterns or holograms of creation that this outpouring is forming and help to create the structures that are being born from them. For as the old patterns of life dissolve and these new ones form, potent new energies are being released. To access and co-create with these energies takes a combination of clear and connected Shakti or a clear flow of life force running through all parts of you, a clear consciousness, an ability to work with light, and a dedicated, pure love light balanced as a feather, allied with a direct connection to the Womb of Creation and the Black Light.

The past pictures of creation have to be released and deleted from your memory banks, body, mind, and soul, in order for the new picture holograms to arise. This may take some letting go, and until you do, the new pictures will not anchor in you, and you will not be able to co-create with them. "This Light is demanding. It forces us to face things as they really are." Love dredges up all that is not love, to be seen and released. It reveals and unites all the polarities we have, bringing our dualities closer and closer together, creating more and more friction and tension until we surrender and reconcile them in the action of love, the light within all life. Once we do, life itself is ready to teach us, if we are ready to receive it and co-create with it as an extension of God/Source, letting go of our old ideas of what God/Source is.

We cannot control, contain, or force this new energy that has no name. We cannot even intellectualize it or work with it in ways that have been successful or worked for us in the past. It is unknown and new, still birthing, still forming, still coming to pass. It is creating a new patterning, a new outpouring, a new picture and palette of creation, a new wave of light that will dissolve most of the old ways of teaching, knowledge, and doing.

We have to change our ways of working in order to work with it, and there are no books or traditions that will tell us how to do this work with life's changing patterns. What we are being asked to do is to bring the light of our own consciousness to work with this awakening light within life so that these primal energies can be creatively channeled to revitalize us and the world.

With the awakening of the Womb of the World's light, the inner structure of life itself is changing, releasing primal creative energies that have not been active since the last great cycle. As they arise again, they give rise to a whole new range of holograms and patterns through which life can flow and the divine can reveal itself in you and the world.

GALACTIC WOMB ALIGNMENT

In 2012–13 and onward the Galactic Womb of the Galactic Center aligns to our planet. This will influence our collective consciousness, the womb of Gaia's consciousness, and each individual's consciousness, and in many cases already is. It will also affect the birthing capacity of women and the abilities and reawakening of the womb center of women. Without this reawakening, a new civilization and way of being cannot be birthed, as all birth comes from the womb. Not just from a Galactic Womb, but from the connection from this to the human womb. Once this connection is re-established, then a thriving new civilization can be (re)birthed. And this awesome responsibility is in the hands of women, especially women who tap in to the fourth spiral.

The womb center of our galaxy emanates out umbilical cords resembling the spiraling structure of DNA, nourishing and connecting all within its system, just as umbilical cords from the placenta of our mothers connected to us. These cords connect us all to the black hole, the Galactic Womb, at the center of our galaxy. Astronomers discovered this black hole in 2002, yet its presence, importance, and connection to Source have been known to the Mayans, Indians, and Egyptians for many thousands of years.

The Mayans call this cord of connection the Kuxan Suum, a lifeline of vibration and communication connecting us from our navel through a spiraling energetic umbilical cord to the Galactic Center, the Womb of Creation. This reconnection is set to more fully align to Earth by 2012, the end of time according to the Tzolkin, the Mayan calendar. In India this umbilical cord or Tortoise Tube connects the God Vishnu through his lotus-shaped navel into the Padmanabhi, the lotus center, or Galactic Center, where he dreams creation into being. In Egypt the god Khonsu acts as the umbilical cord to the Galactic Center, known as the all-powerful, "hidden" god Amun, the god of the most powerful priesthood in Egypt.

All these traditions actively tapped in to the Galactic Center through ceremony and ritual that were known to the leaders and priesthood of their societies. This was all done for the benefit of their society, to keep them in alignment with the Divine Mother and the center of creation.

For a woman, the womb, or *hara,* is the direct connection point to the Galactic Center and beyond. Each individual womb is the connector, the gateway, into the whole. The Galactic Center is not outside of us: it is within the dreaming space of our hearts and wombs united. Each person has this connection inside them, and each person can activate this.

The Galactic Center and its transmissions are not accessed through the mind but rather through your primordial creative center in unison with the mind with the womb guiding the mind to be its transmitting agent or servant. Today the possibility is for all of humanity to access this core of wisdom, love and power directly for themselves without intermediary. Once the connection is established it is always there. Yet to access this requires healing of all the severed and damaged cords, and then a reconnecting and remembering.

Galactic Center is the source of this galaxy, from where this galaxy is birthed. It is where all humans have come from and where we shall all return to. It is a source of unconditional love wed with power in an unlimited state, the beginning and the end, the return back to your Original Self. It is what connects and unifies all parts of yourself. Much wisdom lies in the Galactic Center for humanity and is readily accessed through our primordial creative connection: love, joy, and power united, or womb/hara and heart united.

This is not a transcendent teaching, out there in the cosmos somewhere. Being human and divine without separation or splitting them apart is what is being asked of us. The wisdom and loving power contained in the Galactic Center is rapidly accelerating our evolutionary process, as it reconnects us to our first breath, our first cell, the first cellular division that occurs when one becomes two. The Galactic Center is the home of your soul, where male and female are in union, held in an infinite space of fertile possibility, rich in any potential. It is the highest Tantra and union.

Anything can be created here, and through the womb/hara co-creation in this space is possible and indeed has been done many times in our past. It is the home of your wildest dreams come true once aligned to the natural, innate heart impulse of giving, and your passionate connection to the joyous life force: Shakti.

Galactic Center is a vast yet intimate space, peaceful but incredibly creative and ever changing. It is the ground of being, still and silent, yet containing the surging exciting bliss and power of creativity within itself. Most people who experience their reunion with the Galactic Center describe it as unconditionally loving, accepting, and supporting of every part of themselves, as it gives us what we need. In this sense it is our Mother, the Galactic Womb that nourishes us. The return of this energy now, set to culminate and fully align in 2012, is also the return of the Mother in all her glory. It is the homecoming.

As we journey deeper we experience Galactic Center as a simultaneous experience of being creator and co-created. One can experience oneself creating the world over and over again and seeing humanity creating itself over and over again throughout all the different epochs of history. It is here we realize our power as creators, and it is here that we can manifest this in ways that are unimaginable now. For the Galactic Center is the breath of God, inside and out, and it leads us to the pool of infinite creativity that we live in every day as we create everything moment by moment.

Your heart, womb, and hara are the gateway to the Galactic Center. It is you, and you are it. It is the black in the heart of light and the blinding illumination found in the deepest recesses. It is from here that all grids and reconnections to the web of life are held, and it is here that our ultimate reconnection lies.

Within Galactic Center is held the healing of all our ancestors and the remodeling of our DNA into a new human being. Within it, within you, is held the direct living experience of what it is to be a co-creator with the Creator. This is a living experience that is accessed through the Shakti Circuit Retreats, when you are ready to co-create with the wisdom of the womb within.

RESURRECTION OF SELF IN THE GALACTIC CENTER

In the actual experience of immersion in the Galactic Center we can become annihilated. Black holes literally absorb all light that comes into them, to bring you into Black Light. All parts of you that are still attached will arise to be seen, and the immense love here will break down your constructs. When you are ready to immerse all of yourself into Galactic Center, you will find that even your hard-won soul awareness has to be given up.

To enter this space with every part of yourself means the annihilation of ego and soul and the consequent resurrection of your self. This resurrection and death is an octave higher than before. Whereas before your ego died to resurrect with the soul as its master in the dark night of the soul, here the soul surrenders, dying a death so it can be mastered by God. Now it is God moving through you, with the soul as the servant.

Many highly evolved beings and stellar intelligences of great light live near the frequency and emanations of the Galactic Center. Some of them can withstand the high pressure and intensity of its emanations and then modulate and share energy with humanity in differing forms that we can handle and absorb safely. Some of these waves emanating from Galactic Center are surfacing as new healing modalities.

Galactic Center is in direct alignment with Earth in 2012, as stated by the Mayan Calendar, which will initiate a new phase of evolution for humanity. To master this state, we have to travel through the intense energies of time and all our experiences in all our lifetimes.* This is a powerful journey that all of us are taking right now, combining many lifetimes of experience to integrate them all in order to be present to this ending of a huge Galactic Cycle and the beginning of another. In this process we learn to live in the present, bringing every part of ourselves back together again, weaving ourselves into the web of life. In doing so we become conscious co-creators and live our soul purposes fully, giving freely of our gifts to humanity.

The Galactic Center's infinitely dense point of concentrated mass is a singularity—a total one-pointed focus. This is the goal of many meditation practices and, as stated earlier, is known in sacred geometry as the Bindu point, where all aspects of consciousness, all parts of the fragmented mind-body and soul, all wounds and misperceptions, converge into this one-pointed focus. As this occurs, a new earth and a new form of human being can emerge, as we re-enter the Great Singularity from where we all come.

Continual Birthing

Continual birthing is birthing yourself in each and every moment. This birthing allows us to continually re-create ourselves and to birth anew.

---

*This is similarly discussed in my book *The Power of Shakti,* pages 175–76.

In letting go of every past moment, and embracing the newness of the present moment, we come into the power to create who we are, what we want to express and share with others.

In the experience of being reborn in every moment, we have the power to choose again who we are, what we feel, what we think, and how we choose to respond to the same situation that is presented to us. We can seize this moment and allow the birthing to take place. This birthing sets in motion a whole stream of new moments, each moment holding infinite possibilities for new creations and new ways of being.

Continual birthing is how we co-create with this infinitely creative wave. We realize and we choose again and anew as we align to this subtlest, yet most powerful creative flow as it manifests itself through the dynamism and transparency of living form. It dissolves that which you no longer have need for, and which limits. It conceals that which you know you have but which has yet to manifest in your life. It reveals that which accelerates your evolution with the unexpected meeting, person, event, or situation.

It flows through us, vibrating our bodymind at 570 trillion Hz per second. We are moving incredibly fast every single second of our lives—we are just not aware of it. We are birthing and rebirthing every single moment, moving with this wave, this dance happening all the time. It is the threadlike link between the material and the formless realms, flowing through us and all things perpetually, without ceasing.

Continual birthing in the Galactic Center shows the Wheel of Life, the "hollow bone, the sacred hoop" through which life sings us, through which Spirit moves, through which the song is sung through the conduit of our bodies. This is the "everything and nothing," the magic of nothing working within the loving field of everything. (For more information, see my book, *The Power of Shakti*.

These primal energies are still in flux; they have not yet constellated into new patterns. Only by bringing our own awakened consciousness, the consciousness that asks, "What will love do now?" and joining it with the awakening consciousness within life and the primal energies of creation will we find the information we need.

This is spontaneous knowing, free of thought or form, alive in the moment, fluid and open. This is how Shakti flows and acts, without reference point, past or future. We know everything that we need to sustain ourselves; we know how to evolve and how to regenerate and re-create ourselves, and because we *can* live in a continual response to the divine moment, we know what is needed in each moment, even if our minds do not, *if* we listen and attune ourselves in each moment. If this means being wrong and backtracking on our habitual, outmoded, and dated responses, so be it: humility is part of the spontaneous moment and the gateway into clear communion with the light within life.

This is co-creation: the interaction of our individual light and the world's light in the play of the one light of love. This is the new patterning, the new hologram of creation born from the Black Light, the arising from the Womb of the World. Can you step up and be part of this new patterning in order to be a co-creator with the Universe as it reinvents itself again at a higher octave of love? That is the challenge before each and every one of us now.

12
The End of the Game

The State of Adulthood

To make the move from the child, lost in the sense of I me mine, get get get, take take take, need need need, preoccupied with its own suffering, how they don't have and didn't get the family, job, partner, body, money, fame that they need or ought to have had, and focusing on means to get this—focused on yourself, repeating the same trancelike pattern, reconfirming, needing something from others to make you grow, evolve. This is the state of the human race and almost all of the spiritual community, still tied into mother, childhood conditioning, suckling the teat.

ATTAINING SELF-RESPONSIBILITY

Moving from the child into the mature adult human, one becomes self-responsible, no longer a victim, and able to say no to anything in life. Financially, emotionally and mentally independent, one relates from a place of clarity, not governed by needs. More concerned with giving without conditions, this becomes the basis for soul realization. You work with others to create a better world/better dream state. You explore in joy, fun, and feel gratitude daily. You live in integrity and honor, flow, and effortless manifestation.

You turn back toward the children to bring them into adulthood through various dream state means. You serve others. You seek out all the places where you are still a child tied to mother's/partner's strings, tied to Maya's strings, and heal, delete these attachments that create who you think you are. You propel others to reach adulthood. You do not attach to roles and things: they are who you think you are.

This state of adulthood, a state because it is not an abiding reality, then becomes the prerequisite to shift into awakening. There are still elements of the adult state here, but they are no longer adhered to as gospel truth. As nothing has no substance, there is no compulsion or need to do anything, even serve or help others. Your being is not focused on teaching or giving practices, methods, techniques. Relationships become based on no need. You are the teaching, and there is nothing to teach or give. There is nothing to pray to. You do not need anyone to do anything, and you do not need to do anything. You cannot help others: only they can.

SHIFTING INTO AWARENESS

You become reborn into truth. When there is nothing left, all that remains is nothing. Nothing to do, nowhere to go, nobody to be. All that has seemed important has melted. All purpose is gone. The idea of the soul and its purpose too has dissolved. The soul is surrendered, with its ideas of good, beauty, purpose, and assignment.

For most this arises when this purpose is complete, when the soul has completed its contract, its meaning for existing. For others this is the only soul purpose: to go beyond itself, its own identity, no matter how glorious, light filled or radiant this identity is, it is still an identity. All identities have purpose, all masks conceal what lies underneath it, and as long as there is something underneath something else, there is still a ways to go.

The meaning for existing is ascribed a limited purpose, which for children is a major step. For most, this is enough. For others, they know this comes to an end, and everything that has an end has a beginning. Truth has no beginning and end, and therefore the soul is just another mask to wear, a mask that necessarily has to be burned away and surrendered through your own understanding and dissection of even this identity/purpose. Victim or creator? Dark or light? Good or bad? Virtuous or immoral? What is the difference? Each one creates the other. You cannot have a victim without an oppressor, just as you cannot have good without bad.

As long as you are one or the other, you are still one or the other. Truth has no identity, no mask, no reason to be what it is. It has nothing to be grasped at: it is ungraspable. All one can do is destroy all that stands in its way, all that you have created in order to justify it not being here, to make your world fit in, to make it comprehensible, finite, ordered, and acceptable to yourself and others.

From this truth, you are free to follow the currents as they come. From nothing, nothing arises, whereas in the adult state you can access nothing, but something still arises from nothing in order to heal/teach /give. In awakening, all that arises is nothing, and laughter. Precisely nothing is given, and masks necessarily dissolve in the fire of nothing, which is only a fire to somebody pretending to be something. Truth is hilarious and simple.

Womb Wisdom has been pointing toward the birthing process that the womb invites us into, to experience for others and ourselves. If birth exists, then naturally, too, shall we discover death. Where there is one, there will always be the other.

Undress Who You Think You Are

The final step in Womb Wisdom is to simply enter the womb space to die to all that you have believed yourself to be, to lead your awareness into the womb as you would climb into your own death chamber, and begin the sobering journey of undressing who you think you are—not to do this process to get something, or even because we have invited you to do so, but to take on this final challenge because you are more interested in true freedom rather than the spiritual subculture's promise of a happy ever after, the dream.

Working with the opening of the womb and embarking on all the practices that we have shared with you is not the end goal; it is not the final destination. Once you have cleared your womb, opened your mystical seven gates, and shared the journey with your beloved, do not stop there! There is more, and in truth, this is only the beginning. As the womb creates, so does the womb delete the very experience of your self. This is its ultimate purpose: to dissolve all idea and sense of yourself.

THE DISSOLUTION OF SELF

It seems a paradox, that just as you experience all that you have yearned for, you give it away. Yes, because the sensation that you have achieved peace, contentment, love, and/or union are still showing you that you still exist and that you have an agenda. You have a list of what you should get, experience, acquire, attain, or need.

The truth of who you are does not need anything. It does not need a womb, a beloved, or union with Galactic Center. All these thrills are part of the dream state, where you are the leading character. Still subject to pushes and pulls, emotional pangs, and mental resistances regarding me, my life, and how it should be.

So to fully move to the next step, we invite you to drop everything that you have learned here, and with other teachers. Drop your practices, forget your intentions, let go of your spiritual wisdom, any ideas that you may have surrounding what all this should be looking like.

As you enter your womb, lie in the space as if suspended and freely moving. There is nothing holding you, nothing guiding you, you are alone in this dissolving chamber.

Dissolving the Self

1. Begin by undressing and removing the veil that is your name. Watch it peel off and completely dissolve, never to be found

again. Feel the energy of your name be drawn out of your cells and siphoned out of the part of your brain that stores your identity. Dissolve the sound of your name so you do not recognize it when it is spoken.

2. Move into all the labels that define you: Mother, Father, Daughter, Son, Sister, Brother, Lover, Girlfriend/Boyfriend, and watch them drift past you into nothingness.
3. Begin to detach from any definitions surrounding your work. Let go of what it is that you think you do, your purpose, your position, your contributions, your security, your gifts.
4. Go over all the words that have been used to describe you, undressing these words from your being: intelligent, brilliant, inspiring, beautiful, handsome, fun, loving, kind, impatient, angry, contracted, open, all the words that have once described you, peel them off and dissolve them completely and permanently.
5. See the image of your house burning to the ground, your car, your clothes, your furnishings, your paintings, your music, your decorations, your books, all the things that you have created . . . dissolve them into ashes and then become the dust that blows away.
6. Move into the part of you that believes that you are a certain gender, guide your awareness into loosening the grip that you are female or male. Continue to feel this deeper and deeper until you truly lose sense of the gender identification. Free up all the identification that makes up your sex.
7. Finally, actually allow the mind to open to the realization that you are not even human. Release the idea and makeup of your form, your emotional reactions, all mental ideas and biofeedback; let go of any stored knowledge, spiritual guides, higher self, soul guides, masters, and human needs or reference points.
8. Now, release the part that has been following these guidelines. What happens?

All suffering comes from this sense of "I." Do not add. Take away.

What is left? You are empty. You have no need. Need makes the "I." Relationship proves the "I" and can also bring about its dissolution into union, a union that has nobody involved in it. Where is there interdependence when there is no "I," and how am I connected to you when there is no you?

How can there be any real relationship and union, except when there is no one left to relate to? We only truly relate in the emptiness, for "I" creates all suffering everywhere. All so-called evil, all duality arises from this idea of "I."

In the spaciousness of emptiness where "I" has died, where there is no true self, false self, higher self, lower self, authentic self, inauthentic self, in fact, no self at all, when all else has gone, all ideas, systems, beliefs, and perceptions, one realizes any and all systems are limiting. Following any system slavishly leads to your being a slave. Anything can become a religion . . . anything. Truth needs no system and breaks all systems.

Your core stability is truth that is unchanging and the same for all beings, all genders, all times. Clear the shadow and leave the system. Who you are is beyond any system. Who you are not is within the system.

There is no interrelationship, because there is no "I" to relate to. As there is nobody here, there is nothing to relate to. Only when there is no "I" is there union. Still, identity is the drug of choice for the masses. Death to you and all you believe and stand for should be your battle cry!

Transformation is all about death. Without death there is no change of any significance. Let me repeat that. Without a death, there is no change of any significance, importance, depth, dimension, clarity, or permanence *whatsoever.*

And, of course, you are all scared of dying, as you want something, anything to fill up the hole. You are here to get, not to give. You think that the spiritual path will give you something. But it is not meant to. It is designed to take everything away from you, including, but not limited to, the idea of you.

THE IDEA OF YOU

The idea of you is the ultimate belief system. It has been used for millennia and many millions of people have grown, and are still growing, very rich from it. No one ever awoke using dualistic mind to realize nothing. Only nothing is perfect.

The disparate set of personalities and memories that compose *you* float around, rising and falling, appearing and disappearing on the screen of your mind. This then becomes replaced by fantasies of what you are told you should be like, by an endless stream of TV, magazines, spiritual teachers, books, your friends, et al. Then you have even more fantasies, self-generated, of what you would like to have, acquire, get, in order for you to be more happy, satisfied, abundant, loving, free, peaceful, et al.

You seek a unique identity, different to all others, because of vanity. You don't want to be the same as others, to lose your identity, your specialness, to dissolve your boundaries of self into no self. That would mean dropping down into that deep, dark hole of fear, the hole that you avoid within you, the hole around which you build all your constructs of self to avoid being not self: the sacred wound, all because you don't want to be the same as what is around you. Silly, really.

I am special, I am unique, I love myself, I am different, I am virtuous, I am artistic, I am beautiful . . . and on and on the "I" drones on. There is no self to love. By loving it you mire yourself deeper into the dream; although it can be a happy dream, it is still a dream. Fear of death sustains the illusion of the need for self-identity. All actions taken in this realm are fear- and shadow-based, arising from the fear of nonexistence.

So the question needs to be asked: Why are you on the spiritual path?

To get something or to give something? And what is this thing? To feel good, to look good, to be loved by others, to feel that you are doing something right? To be *seen* and respected by others? For power, authority, fame, and fortune? To be appreciated, praised, hugged? To fill the hole within with another belief, idea, or dogma? To make a difference, to save the world, to be a good person? To have mystical experiences? To replicate your drug experiences? To be in bliss? To replace your present idea of life with the thought/hope/belief of something else?

Or is it to die to all of this and to wake up? Determine this yourself. Evolution ends. Accept it. But you can only accept it once you have stepped out of this picture. And then there is no picture. Contentment.

So, how real are you? Within any question lies the answer. Nothing is perfect and nobody is perfect.

What is the need that drives you? What is the desire that propels you?

Death equals change. Then something new can begin. Yet in truth there is no beginning or ending: this is just another dream.

APPENDIX

Frequently Asked Questions

A few sacred women below have gone deeper into their wombs to share with you what they have found, and what they are living as a result of the reclaiming of their Womb Wisdom and power. Each womb is different as each soul is, so different answers to the same questions arise, yet the theme and energy is similar as all wombs are connected both to the web of life and to the one womb of creation.

What does Womb Work do?

When one discovers what the womb is and what it does, it is a miraculous moment. Once this light switch is proverbially flicked on there is no turning back. In the life of the womb we feel, touch, taste, smell, and see, feeling our "true being" inside.

There used to be a phrase, "If you want to tell someone the truth about themselves, make sure you do it with a sense of humor; otherwise they might kill you!" When the womb is speaking the truth there is no need for this guise or pretense of humor, as it is delivered with sensuality, a deep sense of compassion, and loving wisdom. It is like looking a confident woman in the eyes and seeing her receive a compliment with a clear and present "thank you." She knows who she is and what she is about, and she is mature enough to know that she deserves this compliment, receiving it with grace and finesse.

The womb allows the truth to flow more freely without attachment to the outcome. Once the womb is discovered as an oracle of truth, it is easy to impart the truth without attachment or fear, it simply is the truth and the essence of the womb. Discovering the womb mind and wisdom within provides a new way to navigate through life in soft sensuality and vulnerability, which are indeed great strengths.

Discovering the womb and taking those first steps to clear, cleanse, and open its infinite vastness is an essential piece of the healing journey for every woman. Womb Work doesn't "do" anything; it's closer than that. I would say that Womb Work "gives" you everything. It's a discovering, an unveiling, and a remembering. It's the true orientation for a woman to be coming from. It gives us back our true house, our place of being so that we may rise up and into the heart with strong-rooted foundations and a sense of earthly reality. It's the rock upon which we are built.

The womb is the deep silence, the sound knowledge of truth, and the loving embrace that holds us all together as a life-form within all life-forms. The womb reveals to us true sight, deep feeling, and a sense of support and belonging that is second to none. When all else fails in life, the womb remains as that pillar to lean against, that rock to hold on to, and those arms to cry in.

The womb is a part of the soul embodied here on Earth deep within the human form. Without a doubt it is a woman's most reliable, trusted, and safe home. During the beginning stages of Womb Work, this will become her most precious and treasured discovery. It is the place that does not move, and you will discover a part of yourself that is eternal, ever present, and easily reached.

The difference between the soul and the womb is that the womb is physical, located in the body and a part of the body that women know so well. The soul at first is seemingly etheric, out of reach, and non-physical. But they both merge in the human form through the womb.

What does the womb lead to?

The womb leads us inside to the vast space of the universe within. To have this activated allows us to become a voyager into the unknown of all creation. It leads us to our true being, the massive inner universe that we all possess, yet have completely ignored until now. It leads to clear, present and confident communication and interaction with others. It leads to a new sense of knowing and feeling, not thinking so much as a deep, deep understanding of how things really are. It is the Grail or oracle within that has the answer to each and every question one could ever have. As a result of this new knowing, the womb steers us to places that we would have only have dreamed of before. It is the ultimate manifestation tool for creating the life we have been born to live. It allows us to rebirth ourselves into the truth and majesty of our being and what we are here to do in this life.

The womb leads us to the seed of our being, our first creative spark. It invites us to be reborn, regenerated, and resurrected. It is a cave of pure creativity where we are the creator. The womb is your inner council where you will discover your doctor, surgeon, adviser, confidant, sage, decision-maker, and artist. Every face and facet of your being has roots into the womb, and the womb is the clearest domain to have that meeting.

Ultimately the womb leads us to the womb of all life, the beginning and the end of all known and unknown universes. It is the place upon which all of life simply must travel through to be created. When you realize this, you can begin to create within your own womb, placing projects and heart's desires within its field to be birthed into the world.

Transmuting with the womb is another "gift" of the womb. The womb has the facility to be able to contain and transmute negative or harming energies, stripping away the orientation of the negativity into a pure state of neutrality. This stage of working with the womb comes only after it has been cleared and with the guidance and instruction of a womb teacher.

As a woman, how does it feel to have the womb open?

To have the womb open feels like a precious gift has been given for you to treasure. It is as though a sacred fire has been reignited inside of you, a fire that brings life, power, creation, and passion into your being again. It makes one much more able to discern people, places, and situations more clearly and also more discerning with whom one would want to let into this newly consecrated sacred space. Having the womb open is like having a new stream of vitality pulsing through you. One feels virginal again, as though everything in this sacred sexual area has been born anew. As a result of this newfound virginity and indeed deep knowing and wisdom, a new maturity sprouts into being and one feels truly alive, vivacious, confident, and fertile with possibility.

To live with your womb open brings you a gift and state of being that was previously unknown. You feel beautiful, gorgeous, rich, and sensual without the "edge" of threat perceived from other women. You are non-threatening in your beauty and happiness within your body. You ooze nature, life, promise, and pure joy.

There is a sense of belonging to nature, to the whole world, and that belonging naturally extends to all other life. Again, I could even extend to say that living from the womb is a life lived without fear. Duality dissolves, there is an inherent "rightness" about life and this ease of being is seen, felt, cherished, and hopelessly given to all.

However, an open womb also comes with a self-responsibility as its magnificence is very attracting and will draw attention. During the beginning stages it is advised to place yourself within healthy and productive environments and situations. As you progress, you can begin to turn around seemingly negative situations and places back into a non-harming coexistence with the rest of all life.

What does she feel like for others around you and in relationships?

From my personal experience it is like writing your life in lower case and suddenly someone points out the shift button on the keypad and your life goes from small lower case letters to large capitals at the press of a button. Life goes from being small and ordinary to vast, expansive, and larger than life! My friends and close relatives have commented on how much more at ease I seem to be with myself and life. It is like the womb is in the driver's seat packed full of wisdom for any given situation or circumstance. I seem more confident, more wise, more alive and vibrant and able to take on any situation that may have previously sent me reeling. There is a new calmness and confidence to my demeanor and a knowingness in my eyes that scares boys, yet intrigues real men.

There is an air of confidence and a deep eternal look within the eyes. When engaging with others, you are 100 percent present and searching deeply into their eyes for the truth of where they are coming from. This can seem disconcerting and perhaps make people feel exposed or naked as the whole of that other person is being seen. There is no hiding place or veiling as all is witnessed not from a place of making things right but simply from an angle of seeing the truth of what is before you. Yet this very level of presence lays down a carpet of safety and a sense of being held. Others feel they are being really listened to, that there is another there with them. People eventually relax, open, and allow past hurts, memories, and agonizing mind states to be spoken of, released, and let go.

I have now realized that there is no more socializing left for me; all of my being is now given to holding this space for others. I have no desire to waste time with meaningless conversation anymore.

What feelings arise from the womb and its voice?

Feelings of loving softness, deep knowing, heartfelt compassion, and crystal clarity of perception of any given situation. Also a deep sense of belonging and feeling comfortable in your own skin. I once said that when you have a child, your spectrum of feelings broadens from 10 to 100 on the scale. Everything just expands and feelings become more intense and new. When the womb is open and activated this spectrum of feelings is then accelerated to 1,000 on the scale, and new sensitivities arise; one feels more psychic, more in tune, and more authentic. It is your new voice!

It is the soft feminine voice we have been taught to ignore or invalidate. It is the true voice of all of us waiting to be unveiled, discovered, and heard. As this voice wakes from its ancient slumber, it is soft and quiet, hardly recognizable as a voice and then murmur by murmur, whisper by whisper it increases in volume, and then you hear it for the very first time. It is like the wise voice of your grandmother steeped in ancient wisdom, and it is so familiar you feel like saying "Oh it's you!" And it really is you, the real *you*!

The feelings of the womb are of vastness, eternity, and a silence that is brimming with the light of creation. It includes the world but is not of the world. It reaches all the way into the Galactic Center. It encompasses all of life living, being born, and dying. It can give rise to feelings of softness, yet power, aloneness, and also belonging, tenderness, and bravery. It is the voice of God and also the human. It is the mother and the child. It is birth and even death. It is ancient and also unborn.

You cannot say what it is, as its definitions will always escape you. You can simply rest in the truth that its feelings and voice are all.

Why is the womb important?

It is the greatest secret of secrets that women hold. We have been taught to ignore this powerful center of creation and now it is time to lift the veils of illusion and for everyone to experience and see their true power, beauty, and wisdom! It's the only way to really live, as we are taken from a spectrum of the five senses into the spectrum of several others. Once activated, a morphic field becomes visible and with practice this can be developed to see quite clearly around everything and everyone.

Seeing this morphic field is what is important and possible for things to manifest into our third-dimensional reality. It is so important to break free from the Maya of illusion and know that we create everything from this center inside of us, which then projects out to create our reality on the outside world. Once the womb is discovered we realize that we are completely and without question the true creators of our own lives, reality, and experience. This takes us into a sacred space of complete self-responsibility, which takes us from playing victim to playing creator, our true authentic selves.

A sense of beauty and harmony is restored into one's being and a deep sense of appreciation for the feminine in life, the arts, music, joy, beauty, fertility, and sound. There has been a concerted plot to shut down the visibility of these morphic fields in humanity for a long time so as to make it easier for us to be controlled and steered into the darkness of illusion. The womb is the key to seeing and experiencing a beautiful new reality that has always been innately ours.

It is essential that a woman be taken to the fullness of her being. Living without the womb is like living without the soul. Without the open womb, life will only exist, not be lived through. It simply has to be known, discovered, and entered. Its importance is transmuting clear sight, creating fields of energy that regenerate yourself and your partner in lovemaking, connecting to the web of life and this foundation deep within your being.

Without these elements woman will be tossed around upon the ocean of life, with little soulful direction or sense of orientation. Woman, especially the Western woman, who is mostly head-centered, will be held within the grip of Maya, falling for all its games.

The most important reason I saved for last. A clear and open womb is the channel for the next generations of humankind to come through. By giving birth to new souls here on earth, I can say with the whole of my being that this is one of the surest ways to elevate the future of mankind. Birthing through the open and healed womb, nurturing and rearing with a mother with an open womb, and growing up in an environment where your child sleeps and rests within the field of the womb will and can be a life lived with only instinctive fears ever being experienced. That being will grow into an adult faster than the rest of us and be part of a new generation that heralds in the New Humanity.

The voice of the womb, Anu Ra, speaks:

I am Anu Ra, I am the voice of the womb, the life force and generator of images, experiences, and reality for my own universe. I am the *I am* of it all, the center of creation for everything that my body sees, feels, hears, touches, and tastes. It all comes from this beautiful black, velvety, vast void of nothingness inside me, pure potential waiting to explode into being with the spark of a single glimmer of consciousness.

For many eons of time I have stayed silent, like a wisewoman, waiting for others to have their turn at the creation game. I have been patiently silent, as I have known that this time would come again to speak my truth. Much like a mother watches her child make mistakes and silently sits back so that the child can learn from the experience, I have withheld my voice for I have known that the masculine had to take its turn in the creation game and see that it cannot work and sustain life on its own. The masculine needs the feminine and now I return with love, compassion, and forgiveness for it is time to unite once more to create the balance that manifests unity.

Voyaging through my inner vastness turns perception on its head and allows a new reality to be experienced, the one true reality of pure potential, creativity, and beauty. You will come to realize that everything that is experienced on the outside actually comes from my deep space within. When you venture and voyage inside this inner vastness, you will see many "big bangs" as the light of your consciousness creates whole new worlds and realities waiting to be experienced and explored.

The voice of the womb, Anaiya, speaks:

I speak of a time to come, where humankind will live as love unhindered by fear. A time where we can all give endlessly without wanting, a time where mankind is a gift to the planet and a guide to other lifeforms, where beings will radiate with a light that joyfully sings out into the Universe, where man and woman can give themselves to each other without the fear of losing themselves. They will already be lost, lost in the love of the Divine and their Divinity within each other. There truly will be a time when love will saturate the mind and drench every footstep taken.

And the absolute truth is that this . . . is but one choice away.

Resources

Womb Wisdom is an experiential journey and process. For a complete understanding and more information about the womb and its energetic circuit, known as the Shakti Circuit, please read *The Power of Shakti* (Inner Traditions, 2009). In particular, I would like to point you toward the sections called "The Power of the Womb" and "The Ovaries," which are also available online as an e-book.

For more information visit the authors' websites:

www.padmaaon.com or **www.christblueprint.com**

To access womb healings, click on the "Healing" link. To access Shakti Circuit or Womb Wisdom workshops and retreats, click on the "Events" link.

ABOUT THE WOMB HEALINGS

Some of the specific healings available on the authors' websites, such as the placenta healing, are mentioned in this book. Several other healings relating to the womb are also described on the websites, including a healing for the amygdala and a womb/hara lock. Thousands of people have already received these healings, and their lives have shifted as a result. You can access all of these healings and more on the websites. We would love to hear from you.

ABOUT THE RETREATS

These retreats are powerful and direct experiences. Many of the practices and wisdom shared in these two books are available in these retreats and are integrated and anchored deeply into the womb and bodymind through timeless and enlightening practices from the Egyptian, Aramaic, Hebrew, and tantric traditions of the East. These lineages hold the resonance and space for the retreats and guide retreat participants as an active presence. These retreats are done in Europe and the United States.

Once you experience one of these retreats, you will understand in your very cells and DNA what the womb is and what it can do. The resonance and loving power of these retreats can open you to your essence and connection to the Galactic Center, the womb and heart of this galaxy. They are not intellectual teachings, as the retreat's core purpose is to bring people into their direct knowing. They are deeply transformative.

Namastute.

Acknowledgments

I would like to thank my beloved Anaiya for being with me, for loving, and for having the dedication to burn through the shadow of the spirals with love and passion. I thank all the women and men who contributed in some way to this book through their healing and willingness to transform. I thank Laura Re for her initial help and for the piece "The Voice of the Womb." Thank you to Jon Graham at Inner Traditions for being open, and feeling what this is all about.

Padma Aon Prakasha

I would like to thank my womb for welcoming this arduous, wondrous journey, and my heart for having the capacity to withstand these trials and healings. I would also like to thank my shadow for being such a good sport.

None of this would have been possible without the guidance, challenges, support, and love from my beloved Padma, who walked alongside me every step of the way. It has only been possible through our reverence of the feminine that these paths and maps have revealed themselves again so that every woman has access to this sacred essence within. To all our readers, I say one last thing: Tap in to this loving wisdom, because it is there for you, silently and patiently waiting within the cave of your heart.

Anaiya Aon Prakasha

Index

BOOKS OF RELATED INTEREST

The Power of Shakti
18 Pathways to Ignite the Energy of the Divine Woman
by Padma Aon Prakasha

Moonrise
The Power of Women Leading from the Heart
Edited by Nina Simons with Anneke Campbell

The Temples of Light
An Initiatory Journey into the Heart Teachings of the Egyptian Mystery Schools
by Danielle Rama Hoffman

Shamanic Breathwork
Journeying beyond the Limits of the Self
by Linda Star Wolf

Shakti
Realm of the Divine Mother
by Vanamali

The Triple Goddess Tarot
The Power of the Major Arcana, Chakra Healing, and the Divine Feminine
by Isha Lerner

The Great Goddess
Reverence of the Divine Feminine from the Paleolithic to the Present
by Jean Markale

The Woman with the Alabaster Jar
Mary Magdalen and the Holy Grail
by Margaret Starbird

INNER TRADITIONS • BEAR & COMPANY
P.O. Box 388
Rochester, VT 05767
1-800-246-8648
www.InnerTraditions.com

Or contact your local bookseller